Digital Cultures

The book explores contemporary selfie-taking practices; digital experiences of love, romance and infidelity; sexting rituals; self-tracking habits; strategies used by the Internet famous; and the power of hashtag campaigns and memes in espousing a cause. Rejecting binary narratives on digital cultures, it showcases the fascinating ways in which we use our digital devices, social media platforms, and apps by drawing upon academic research, everyday observations and a determination to challenge assumptions and hasty generalizations. It also engages with emerging narratives on online authenticity, privacy, digital detox, and the digital divides prevalent both in India and abroad.

Smeeta Mishra is a communication and media studies faculty who has taught at various educational institutes in India and abroad including IIM Calcutta, IIM Ahmedabad, and Bowling Green State University, Ohio. After completing her PhD from the University of Texas at Austin, she has been researching how digital technology mediates our identities, relationships, and everyday practices over the last 15 years. She is currently associate professor at the Xavier Institute of Management, Bhubaneswar.

Routledge Focus on Management and Society
Series Editor: **Anindya Sen**, *Professor of Economics, Indian Institute of Management Calcutta, Kolkata, West Bengal, India*

The invisible hand of market has today been replaced by the visible hand of managerial capitalism. As the power and role of the managers have expanded, the world also has become more dynamic and volatile. To run their organisations more efficiently, the managers need to be aware of new developments taking place all around them. The Focus series addresses this need by presenting a number of short volumes that deal with important managerial issues in the Indian context. Volumes in the series will cover topics not only of perennial interest to managers but also emerging areas of interest like neuro marketing. Some of the well-established areas of research like bottom-of-the-pyramid marketing will be dealt with specifically in the Indian context, as well as critical developments in other fields, like Auction Theory.

The series is designed to introduce management theorists and researchers (as well as the lay public) to a diverse set of topics relevant directly or peripherally to management in a concise format, without sacrificing basic rigour.

Other Books in this series

Understanding Auctions
Srobonti Chattopadhyay and Rittwik Chatterjee

Neuromarketing in India
Understanding the Indian Consumer
Tanusree Dutta and Manas Kumar Mandal

Strategic Change and Transformation
Managing Renewal in Organisations
Swarup K Dutta

Excellence in Supply Chain Management
Balram Avittathur and Debabrata Ghosh

For a full list of titles in this series, please visit: https://www.routledge.com/Routledge-Focus-on-Management-and-Society/book-series/RFMS

Digital Cultures

Smeeta Mishra

LONDON AND NEW YORK

First published 2021
by Routledge
2 Park Square, Milton Park, Abingdon, Oxon OX14 4RN

and by Routledge
52 Vanderbilt Avenue, New York, NY 10017

Routledge is an imprint of the Taylor & Francis Group, an informa
business

British Library Cataloguing-in-Publication Data
A catalogue record for this book is available from the British Library

Library of Congress Cataloging-in-Publication Data
A catalog record for this title has been requested

ISBN: 978-0-367-72498-6 (hbk)
ISBN: 978-0-367-72539-6 (pbk)
ISBN: 978-1-003-15522-5 (ebk)

Typeset in Times
by Deanta Global Publishing Services, Chennai, India

For Rajesh and Samaira

Contents

Preface

One day my students forwarded me a meme they had made after I completed teaching my last class in a communication course at a management school in eastern India. It drew upon a popular scene from a Bollywood movie titled *Three Idiots* in which "Virus" (Dr. Viru Sahastrabuddhe, the college's strict director) gives a special pen to a student called "Rancho" played by Aamir Khan, the protagonist of the film.

I had just thanked the class representative for all the work he had done during the semester. As a token of appreciation, I had given him a small gift. The little packet had some chocolates inside. I told the class the packet contained something that kept me motivated to complete my dissertation during my Texas days. They clapped for him and one of the students had taken a picture of us. Within a few minutes, they had created the meme and circulated it.

The idea for this book emerged from my participant observation in such digital cultural practices. The inspiration to write on digital cultures came from my research as well as teaching engagements. Researching in this area for nearly 15 years has shown me that we need to probe deeper to understand the ways in which various people use digital technology, social media platforms, and apps.

This book is a product of my desire to connect everyday observations about digital practices with academic research in relevant areas. I wanted to make academic research accessible to multiple audiences. My goal was to bring out the intricacies and subtleties associated with the usage of digital technology and social media using a conversational style but without compromising on academic rigor.

Apart from my research, watching everyday digital practices amongst my students continually kept me abreast of Gen Z perspectives. Although many people in my generation and those older than me often blame young people for "wasting time" on social media or for being "self-obsessed," I found that they use it for a variety of purposes that are meaningful to them.

Of course, not all of it is purposeful. Nor is that their intention. But I found that there is more to some selfies, memes, online relationships, self-tracking practices, and online campaigns than what appears on the surface.

In this book, I strive to analyze the contemporary focus on the visual, digital experiences of love, romance and infidelity, our self-care and wellness rituals, practices of the Internet-famous and new manifestations of authenticity and engagement. I hope that the insights presented here will help us challenge some of our assumptions about digital cultural practices and facilitate the emergence of a more nuanced understanding of people's digital and social media engagements.

Acknowledgments

My heartfelt thanks to Professor Anindya Sen for making me believe that the COVID-19 pandemic could not stop the flow of anybody's words including mine. I would also like to thank Taylor & Francis for giving me the opportunity to do what I love doing – writing about digital cultures. A big thank you to my students, past and present, for keeping me intrigued about their digital practices both inside the classroom and outside it. Finally, I want to thank my husband, Rajesh, for being the first person to read the chapters in this book. And thank you, dear Samaira, for adding meaning to all that I do.

Introduction

The village council of Madora, a hamlet located near Mathura, announced a fine of Rs. 21,000 for any woman who was seen talking on her mobile phone in public. The goal was to restrict interaction between woman and men as the council believed it was leading to socially unacceptable romantic liaisons and elopements (Agence France-Presse, 2017). Many villages in the north Indian states of Uttar Pradesh and Haryana have been wary about women using cell phones.

While such practices draw upon deeply patriarchal beliefs and values in Indian society, paranoia about the impact of new technology and new inventions is nothing new. Even Socrates was deeply worried about the invention of the alphabet. He thought it would make men and women forgetful as they would stop relying on memory and depend on the written word instead (Baym, 2015).

Similarly, in the late 19th century, the accessibility offered by electrical communication made many anxious. People were apprehensive that they would no longer be able to keep "private family secrets" as the "telephone men" would be able to hear all private conversations people had over the telephone (Marvin, 1988, p. 68). While telephones led to the leaking of family secrets, they also led to the creation of new ones as they facilitated unlikely courtships among young men and women leading to much social anxiety. Of course, not everyone was pessimistic about the usage of telephones and believed it would lead to a more democratic and accessible society.

The fact is that people often bestow new inventions and technology with the power of singularly bringing about far-reaching changes without exploring the context in which specific types of usages occur. For instance, some argued in the late 19th century that with the increased usage of electricity for cooking, there would be no failed marriages (Marvin, 1988). Well, the rising divorce rates worldwide bear testimony to how wildly optimistic the early predictions and hopes were.

Similarly, in the case of digital technology, depending on whether a person adheres to a utopian or dystopian view about it, there is a tendency to attribute all things good or bad to its widespread usage. The impact of new technology on human behavior is painted with broad strokes while ignoring the nuances involved in its diverse usage.

For example, the British television series *Black Mirror*, a dystopian science fiction anthology which was later purchased by Netflix in 2015, highlighted the dark and unanticipated consequences of digital technologies. It became highly popular because people identified with many of the disturbing situations it depicted (Ketchell, 2019). The episodes often took a familiar situation and pushed it to the extreme, creating anxiety and fear about the dark places new technologies might lead us. Of course, we are already witnessing some of the detrimental effects of excessive use of digital technology.

According to Baym, most people have one of the three following perspectives on the relationship between technology and human behavior. There are those who believe in technological determinism and consider technology as a causal agent that creates major changes in society which human beings have little power to resist. Then there are those who take a social construction of technology approach and believe that people are the primary sources of change in society. Finally, those who hold a social shaping of technology perspective believe that technology and society as continually shaping one another. This represents the middle ground.

This book adopts the third perspective. It draws upon the belief that a finer understanding of digital culture must take alternative realities into account and explore the various contexts of Internet and social media usage. It seeks to demonstrate the intricate ways in which we interact with digital devices, apps, and platforms. But before we engage in such a feat, we must ask: Why study digital culture at all?

It is important to engage with digital culture to gain a better understanding of contemporary notions of self, identity, relationships, romance, intimacy, activism, health, etc. Understanding digital culture will also help digital immigrants and digital natives connect better with each other.

Of course, digital culture is an umbrella term. It is difficult to give a specific definition of the term although it is easy to identify what it includes. Digital culture includes every interaction we have with digital technology. It includes our usage of social media platforms and apps, the habit of taking selfies and recording everyday life using digital pictures, forming online communities, using fitness trackers, signing online petitions, tweeting, blogging, vlogging, and so much more. In this book, I focus on some of the most significant aspects of digital culture.

This book weaves both global and Indian events and contexts in the chapters. In fact, the Indian experience presents a unique case. In 2018, India had over 480 million Internet users with a majority of people accessing the Internet through their mobile phones (Keelery, 2020b). It was ranked the second largest online market worldwide in the year 2019. Cheap data packages combined with affordable, Indian language–enabled mobile phones made accessing the Internet easy for many.

However, the overall Internet penetration level in the country stood at just over 40 percent in June 2019 (Keelery, 2020b). The skewed gender ratio and stark rural–urban divide in terms of Internet access complicate the situation and reinforce digital divides. For instance, in the year 2016, the male to female ratio in terms of the number of Internet users in the country stood at 70:30 (Keelery, 2020a).

The level of Internet access amongst women is adversely affected by dominant patriarchal values in Indian society and low literacy rates and digital awareness amongst women. Furthermore, while 66% of India's population live in villages, the Internet density is just 25.3% in rural areas compared to 97.9% in urban areas (Parsheera, 2019). These numbers are indicative of the varied and complex digital cultural practices prevalent in the Indian context.

I started researching on online cultures in 2006 when I was teaching at Bowling Green State University, Ohio. Specifically, my research over the past 15 years has focused on media convergence, online journalism, self-presentation in online environments, visual presentation on social media, and online health communication, amongst others. In 2008, I developed a course titled "Online Communication" while I was teaching at the Indian Institute of Management Ahmedabad (IIM-Ahmedabad). In 2014, I co-authored a book titled *Online Communication for Managers* along with Prof. MM Monippally, a retired professor of Communication at IIM-Ahmedabad.

My continued interest in digital cultures led me to offer an elective titled "Social Media, Identity and Culture" to students in the flagship MBA program at the Indian Institute of Management Calcutta. The rich discussions in the classroom enriched my understanding of contemporary digital cultures. The students facilitated my exploration of various aspects of digital culture from multiple vantage points instead of limiting myself to perspectives influenced by my own training and background.

The goal of this book is to give the reader a critical understanding of how social media influences and is influenced by our sociocultural contexts. The book seeks to engage with various aspects of social media communication and apply them to an understanding of the role of social media in our everyday lives. Finally, I hope that the reader applies the insights gained from this book to her online–offline communication, identity practices, and multimedia engagements.

Each chapter strives to locate answers to a few questions and poses new questions as well. Chapter 1 titled "Exploring Selfies – Beyond 'Duckfaces' and Adolescent Rituals" examines one of the most common facets of digital culture: Taking and posting selfies on social media platforms. This chapter also analyzes the beliefs and assumptions behind certain selfie-taking practices. It highlights the allegations of narcissism leveled against selfie-takers, primarily women, who are often disciplined for taking too many selfies.

This chapter emphasizes the nuanced contexts in which selfies are taken, posted, liked, and commented upon. Different sociocultural contexts, individual situations, and types of digital platforms influence the nature and composition of selfies. Rejecting the binary narrative that selfies are either empowering or disempowering for the selfie-taker, this chapter takes the reader on a journey of alternative selfies including domestic violence selfies, rape survivor selfies, illness selfies, armpit hair selfies, nude selfies, and funeral selfies, amongst others.

Overall, the chapter highlights the need to treat selfies as a new visual language without judging selfie-taking practices based on our own perspectives and assumptions. While attempting to understand selfie-taking practices, it is also pertinent that we venture beyond the selfies people post on mainstream digital platforms such as Facebook, Twitter, and Instagram and strive to engage with the ones posted in pseudonymous and anonymous online environments.

Going beyond individual identities and selfies, Chapter 2 titled "'Send me a sexy picture': Love, Intimacy and Infidelity in the Digital Era" deals with our romantic relationships including contemporary hook-up cultures, mobile dating apps, and the new ways in which we express love and intimacy online. It delves into contemporary sexting practices and their gendered nature. As we all know, while a woman is often shamed for sexting, a man is considered adventurous if he engages in similar behavior.

This chapter highlights the need to contextualize sexting practices and not merely focus on sensational cases of sexting gone wrong. One must keep in mind that the youth today are digital natives who consider it both healthy and "normal" to express their feelings online. At the same time, it is important for them to understand the role of consent in sexual communication and expression. Considering the fact that coerced sexting and blackmail can lead to grave consequences, schools and sex education programs can play a critical role in preventing some of them.

Navigating the ambiguous waters of Internet infidelity, this chapter also deals with the million-dollar question many ask today: Am I cheating even if I am not touching my virtual partner? With people making distinction between emotional affairs online and sexual affairs, what comprises online infidelity has become a highly debated issue. The damage caused by online emotional affairs often gets underplayed when "cheating" is reduced to physical intimacy alone. With more people using extramarital apps, online partner surveillance is also on the rise.

Chapter 3 titled "Self-tracking One's Way to Wellness: Expert patients, Quantified Health and Online Communities" illuminates how digital platforms have facilitated the sharing of personal journeys of illness and wellness with the public. Online health communities help people find both information and emotional support although not all of them operate within the boundaries of medical science and some communities such as anti-vaccination forums position themselves in opposition to it. The relationship between patients and doctors is also changing with the latter responding in diverse ways to the informed patient's Google searches about his health and sickness.

The Internet and digital healthcare tools have also contributed to the emergence of the proactive, "digitally engaged" patient and the collection of data on the human body. More people are using self-tracking apps and wearables to track their body functioning and everyday living including aspects such as health, sex, pregnancy, mothering, and more.

Chapter 3 highlights various aspects of the debate on the use of digital tools and self-tracking apps even as governments are also increasingly relying on digital health technology to deal with complex healthcare challenges. While proponents of digital healthcare technologies emphasize how it empowers people, critics draw attention to its surveillance capabilities and discriminatory tendencies including reinforcement of the digital divide.

Overall, this chapter unravels how our understanding of health is transforming with more focus being placed on individual lifestyle changes rather than structural factors at the societal level. This chapter is especially pertinent in times of a pandemic when we need to reflect on whether focus on lifestyle and individual parameters of health is enough to protect populations against disease and death. The COVID-19 pandemic forces us to revisit the role of the state and public hospitals in ensuring the health of populations.

After discussing digital healthcare, we then move on to Chapter 4 titled "Becoming Internet Famous: Performing 'Authenticity' and Engaging Audiences" which deals with Internet celebrities or microcelebrities including YouTube stars and the "Instafamous." This chapter traces the history of Internet celebrities right from the days of Jennifer Ringley, who was the first woman to broadcast her life on the Internet by letting people see her everyday live including sexual acts by installing a webcam on the computer in her dorm room in a US college.

The chapter brings out the dynamic differences between traditional celebrities and microcelebrities and how the latter choreograph "ordinariness" and perform "authenticity" online. I use multiple case studies to highlight the techniques used by microcelebrities to attract and hold attention of their target audiences including those of UK-based beauty vlogger Zoella and controversial gamer PewDiePie.

This chapter also includes an analysis of strategies used by Internet celebrities from India who present a heterogeneous lot including young comedians to senior citizens whose culinary skills have made them famous on YouTube. The Indian case studies include those of CarryMinati, who is famous for his roasts and diss tracks; Mastanamma, Grandpa Kitchen, and Nisha Madhulika who made a name in the food genre; and, All India Bakchod, a Mumbai-based comedy group that met a silent death after years of glory.

An examination of the techniques used by these Internet celebrities dispels the myth that anybody who is famous on the Internet must necessarily bare their private life online. While some microcelebrities do follow that method, others create a narrative of intimacy and relatability using completely different strategies.

Chapter 5 titled "Digital Activism: The Power of Hashtags and Memes" traces the origin of hashtag activism and memes both in India and the world. By drawing upon various case studies including hashtag campaigns such as #BlackLivesMatter, #MeToo, and #IceBucketChallenge amongst others, the chapter demonstrates how hashtag campaigns gather momentum. Compelling personal narratives often help to garner attention but the momentary attention that an issue gets online must be sustained by the digital labor of multiple stakeholders to initiate policy change. Moreover, once an issue garners momentum online, it can easily transfer to the offline world in the form of street demonstrations and protests.

Digital activism in India has come a long way from the days of the Anti-Corruption Movement led by Anna Hazare in 2011 and the Delhi Gang Rape protests in 2012. It is no longer limited to the English-speaking, urban, middle classes. Today, one sees the emergence of a more heterogenous public that posts in regional and local languages on the Internet.

This chapter also highlights the power of memes to start and sustain a conversation on a particular topic, especially in countries such as China which have severe restrictions on freedom of speech and expression.

In India, memes are often inspired by popular dialogues in Bollywood movies. After analyzing various case studies, the chapter identifies the defining features of digital activism, especially its ability to connect local events with global narratives and its capacity to start a public debate on a socially stigmatized topic. It also draws attention to the limits of digital activism.

Finally, Chapter 6 titled "Digital Detox: Untangling oneself from the Web" tells the story of the minority that rejects having social media presence or takes frequent social media sabbaticals for varied reasons. Of course, digital detoxing was more prevalent in a pre-COVID era as the pandemic has made it almost impossible to stay away from the virtual world and social media platforms. This book concludes with a summary of the overarching digital cultural practices and a look at the future.

References

Agence France-Presse (2017, May 3). Rs 21,000 fine for women seen using mobile phone, says UP village. Retrieved from https://www.ndtv.com/india-news/rs-21000-fine-for-women-seen-using-mobile-phone-says-up-village-1689094

Baym, N. (2015). *Personal connections in a digital age*. Cambridge, UK: Polity Press.

Keelery, S. (2020a). Distribution of internet users in India 2016–2020 by gender. *Statista.com*. Retrieved from https://www.statista.com/statistics/750999/india-share-of-internet-users-by-gender/

Keelery, S. (2020b). Number of internet users in India from 2015 to 2018 with a forecast until 2023 (in millions). *Statista.com*. Retrieved from https://www.statista.com/statistics/255146/number-of-internet-users-in-india/

Ketchell, M. (2019). 'Black Mirror': The dark side of technology. *The Conversation*. Retrieved from https://theconversation.com/black-mirror-the-dark-side-of-technology-118298

Marvin, C. (1988). *When old technologies were new: Thinking about electric communication in the late nineteenth century*. New York: Oxford University Press.

Parsheera, S. (2019). India's on a digital sprint that is leaving millions behind. *BBC.com*. Retrieved from https://www.bbc.com/news/world-asia-india-49085846

1 Exploring selfies

Beyond "duckfaces" and adolescent rituals

A "selfie" refers to a picture you take of yourself alone or with other people usually with a cell phone camera and often with the purpose of sharing it on social media. Internet culture researchers, Theresa Senft and Nancy Baym in their now-famous article titled "What Does the Selfie Say? Investigating a Global Phenomenon," identify the selfie as both an object and a practice with the capacity for complex and nuanced communication. According to them, a selfie is a "photographic *object* that initiates the transmission of human feeling in the form of a relationship...A selfie is also a practice—a gesture that can send (and is often intended to send) different messages to different individuals, communities, and audiences" (p. 1589).

As we all know the Oxford English Dictionary named "selfie" as the word of the year in 2013 after it beat "twerk," another buzzword that year referring to the sexually provocative dance move popularized by singer Miley Cyrus (ABC News, 2013). Meanwhile, the first documented use of the word "selfie" has been traced to a post on an Australian online forum in 2002 where a user called "Hopey" wrote about how he tripped and injured his lip in a drunken state and sought advice on whether licking his lips would make the stitches dissolve faster than they should (Liddy, 2013). The text was accompanied by a close-up picture of his swollen lips with black sutures on them. Thus, the word "selfie" has been in use since the year 2002 and transformed from being a "social media buzzword to mainstream short-hand for a self-portrait photograph" as more people started taking their own pictures and posting them on social media (ABC News, 2013).

The word "selfie" also led to several spinoffs such as "helfie" when you focus on your hair in the picture, "belfie" when you focus on your bottom, and "drelfie" when you take a picture of yourself in a drunken state ("'Selfie' coined," 2013). Of course, none of these words have managed to become as popular as the word "selfie."

While self-portraiture has a long history, the "selfie" is a more recent phenomenon reflective of the current fascination with the visual medium.

It is different from previous forms of self-portraiture not only in terms of technique and form but also in the way it is perceived as something spontaneous and casual (Walsh & Baker, 2016). Some selfie researchers, however, question the perception of spontaneity held by people about selfies (Walsh & Baker, 2016). They point that although selfies are portrayed as a photograph taken in the moment, many individuals may opt for multiple takes on a selfie before they decide on just the right one to post on a social media platform.

A visit to a mall or a shopping plaza in any Indian city will give an idea about the number of young men and women working hard on the right angle, the right exposure, and the right facial expressions for their selfies even as they strike just the right pose standing beside glamorous mannequins outside different outlets of well-known brands. Taking selfies and posting them online increased exponentially with the availability of inexpensive camera phones, the popularity of front-facing camera phones, and social media platforms (Senft & Baym, 2015).

Selfies function as a personal branding tool for many. In fact, management scholars have identified 7 primary genres of selfies including autobiography, parody, propaganda, romance, self-help, travel diary, and coffee table book based on an analysis of images on Instagram (Eager & Dann, 2016). Of course, such a classification does not include non-mainstream apps which may produce alternative classifications.

Although much has been written about selfies in general, there is little agreement on the motivations of selfie-takers and the impact of selfies on our lives. While marketers use happy consumer selfies to communicate a hip and youthful message, news media often highlight the harmful effects of selfies including narcissism, body dysmorphia, and psychosis (Senft & Baym, 2015). For instance, an article in *The Atlantic* magazine expresses the confusion surrounding selfies really well:

> Are you sick of reading about selfies? Are you tired of hearing about how those pictures you took of yourself on vacation last month are evidence of narcissism, but also maybe of empowerment, but also probably of the click-by-click erosion of Culture at Large? (Garber, 2014)

Evidently, the term "selfie" and practices associated with it remain a source of controversy and debate even as a resolution any time soon appears unlikely and far-fetched (Senft & Baym, 2015).

This chapter starts with an account of gender stereotypes reflected in some selfies. It then highlights allegations of narcissism that have been leveled at selfie-takers, especially women, even as the impact of selfie-taking habits on their lives has been analyzed by many. The chapter moves on to give an account of alternative perspectives on selfie-taking practices and takes the reader on a journey of exploration of alternative selfies including those by domestic violence survivors, rape survivors, sexual minorities, people who are ill, and those who try to resist normative definitions of beauty and body type. The chapter concludes with the need to avoid giving reductive labels to selfies and selfie-takers and acknowledge selfies as a new form of visual language instead.

Gender stereotypes: "feminine" women and "macho" men

Do men and women pose differently in their selfies? To find an answer to this question, communication researchers Nicole Döring, Anne Reifl, and Sandra Poeschl examined the degree of gender stereotyping in Instagram selfies and then compared it to magazine advertisements.

They found that Instagram selfies not only reproduce gender stereotypes, they do so even more than advertisements in magazines. For instance, the study showed that women may lie down on a couch or strike a kissing pose while men stand solidly on the ground. The researchers claimed that young women often used "visual codes of subordination" identified by previous researchers such as "feminine touch, lying posture, imbalance, withdrawing gaze, loss of control, and body display" and other gender-specific expressions popular on social media such as "the kissing pout implying seduction/sexualization and the faceless portrayal (implying focus on the body solely)" (Döring et al., 2016, p. 961). Meanwhile, young men focused on showing their physical strength and muscles in their selfies.

One of the reasons why the researchers found such a high degree of gender stereotyping could be the method they used to identify selfies for the study. The researchers selected selfies that had general hashtags such as #selfie, #me, or #myself and not those more reflective of women with feminist identities or those belonging to sexual minority groups such as #queerselfie, #transselfie, or #feministselfie (Döring et al., 2016). Here, it must also be mentioned that not all gender stereotypical selfies win "likes" on social media. Döring and her fellow researchers also draw attention to "the line between gender role conformity that is appreciated among young people of different cultures and milieus, and gender stereotyping that is perceived as inauthentic, staged, ridiculous or 'cheap'?" (p. 961). For instance, while the kissing pout is a common pose for young women taking selfies, it is also criticized as "duckface" by many (Döring et al., 2016).

The much-debated "duckface" selfie actually elicits varied responses from people: "Online daters think duck face is hot; college students think duck face means you're a slacker; and scientists think duck face means you're emotionally unstable" (Lebowitz, 2016). The fact is that selfies, especially those of women, are under constant social scrutiny (Shah, 2015). Nishant Shah, a digital research scholar, argues that it is the very nature of selfies as something that is "temporary, multiple, travelling, visible, and public that leads to it becoming an object of shame and control, particularly of women's bodies in the digital spaces" (p. 88).

Selfies also prompt many to try and deduce someone's personality type from the type of selfies they take and post online. The following section discusses the allegations of narcissism often made against selfie-takers.

Selfies and personality types: Allegations of narcissism

When we see someone's Facebook profile full of their own selfies, what is the first thought that comes to our minds? Many of us are likely to assume that the person must be narcissistic. Several researchers have also linked selfie-taking habits with narcissism. For instance, Jesse Fox and Margaret Rooney, both communication researchers at Ohio State University, examined if personality traits could predict social media usage and selfie-taking and editing behaviors among American men and found that narcissistic men reported spending more time on social networking sites. The researchers also found that narcissistic men posted selfies more frequently. Further, the study claimed that narcissists and those high in self-objectification edited their selfies more frequently before posting them on social networking sites.

But does narcissism imply mental illness? Online culture scholars Theresa Senft and Nancy Baym (2015) vehemently reject linking narcissism to any form of mental illness. They point out that even the study by Fox and Rooney mentioned above, which analyzes men's selfie-taking habits using the "Dark Triad" of personality traits including narcissism, Machiavellianism, and psychopathy, refers to a level within the normal range of functioning. Thus, one should be cautious about extreme views which allege that people who take frequent selfies are abnormal in some way.

Many other scholars have also been critical of the increasing linkage made between narcissism and selfie-taking behaviors in popular discourse, especially in news media reports. For instance, Derek Conrad Murray, art history and visual culture expert, laments that the recent debates amongst psychiatrists and psychologists on whether narcissism is an actual personality disorder has not made journalists and scholars from various disciplines more cautious in associating the term with selfie-taking behaviors, especially in women.

Jessica Maddox, a researcher at the University of Georgia, argues that journalists have wrongly adopted the Narcissus story to describe selfie-taking activities. She points out that while most selfie-takers share their images on social media platforms, Narcissus loved himself and his image so much that he would not share it with anyone.

Refuting the allegation that selfies are merely "narcissistic overshares," Alicia Eler, author of *The Selfie Generation: Exploring our Notions of Privacy, Sex, Consent, and Culture*, points out that taking selfies represents just one aspect of our digital lives today. She argues that it's usually men who refer to female selfie-takers as narcissistic due to their own patriarchal conditioning wherein women are regarded as objects to be viewed and photographed rather than as people who can actively take their own pictures. She explains that a woman taking a moment to look at herself is a courageous act in a world that only validates men looking at women. In fact, when a woman looks at her own image in a public space, she risks being considered vain (Eler, 2019).

In all likelihood, Eler's arguments will resonate with women living in patriarchal societies who have experienced the male gaze in public places. In such a situation, it is the woman who is expected to look away even as the man continues to evaluate her. In fact, young women in patriarchal societies are often trained to "ignore" the intrusive male gaze which is considered "normal" and socially acceptable. Eler's claims about society being too critical of women taking selfies also come in the context of researchers and laypersons alike focusing, analyzing, and judging women's selfie-taking habits. The next section will highlight the findings of studies that analyze the impact of selfies on women's lives.

#Killfie: Death by selfie

Selfies have become so ubiquitous that some feel compelled to take a selfie even in dangerous locations and conditions leading to injuries and even death. For instance, a 19-year-old student slipped into raging waters and died while trying to take a selfie standing on the edge of the barrage in the Ganges in Kanpur (IANS, 2016). It had rained and the water levels in the Ganges were high that day. His six friends jumped into the water to save him but all of them were swept away by the current and died. Unfortunately, India witnesses the largest number of such selfie-related deaths in the world based on a study conducted by researchers at the All India Institute of Medical Sciences. Based on an analysis of news reports in English-language dailies, the study indicated that there have been 259 selfie-related deaths between October 2011 and November 2017 (Bansal et al., 2018). About half of these deaths in the 20–29 age group.

More than 70% of people who were killed while clicking selfies were men. The researchers suggest that one could attribute the high number of selfie deaths in India to the fact that the country is home to the world's largest youth population (age <=30) and it's primarily young people who engage in such behavior. A study published in the *Journal of Family Medicine and Primary Care* identified the three primary causes of selfie deaths: (1) drowning, (2) falling from a great height, and (3) being hit by a moving vehicle such as a train or car.

The researchers also cautioned that it is difficult to ascertain the actual number of selfie deaths and we most likely underestimate the number as deaths caused while taking selfies are rarely reported as such. For instance, if a person were killed by a car hitting him while taking a selfie on the road, the incident is more likely to be reported as a car accident than as a death caused by taking a selfie. Various countries have taken measures to prevent selfie-related deaths. For instance, 16 areas in Mumbai have been categorized as "no selfie" zones (Bansal et al., 2018).

Appearance comparisons: Mood and body image issues

Research shows that women upload pictures on social media more frequently than men and invest more time and effort in managing their personal profiles (Stefanone et al., 2011; as cited in Mills et al., 2018). In 2014, a project called "Selfiecity" led by Dr. Lev Manovich, a computer science professor at the City University of New York, examined selfies shared on Instagram in five major cities including Bangkok, Berlin, Moscow, New York, and Sao Paulo and found "significantly more women selfies than men selfies (from 1.3 times as many in Bangkok to 1.9 times more in Berlin)." Moscow proved to be an outlier as the researchers found 4.6 times more female selfies than male selfies.

However, we must be cautious while interpreting such data as it would be erroneous to conclude that what happens in the biggest cities of the world happens in its small towns and villages as well. For instance, the demographics of selfie-takers and the nature of selfies taken in New Delhi and

Mumbai are likely to differ somewhat from selfies taken in an unknown village in the Indian hinterlands. The sociocultural context in which selfies are taken thus becomes an important variable in understanding selfies worldwide.

However, there is little research that highlights the differences in selfie-taking habits between metropolises and semi-urban or rural spaces. Instead, there has been a lot of interest in examining the impact of social media usage on appearance concerns among women, especially in terms of dissatisfaction with their own bodies (Mills et al., 2018). With so many people posting selfies, a comparison of images is inevitable. And, when people start comparing their selfies with those of others, they end up focusing on their physical appearance (Mills et al., 2018).

Jasmine Fardouly, a psychologist in Australia, and her colleagues examined the impact of appearance comparisons on women. They found that women primarily make upward appearance comparisons which involve comparing oneself with someone more attractive than them. They also found that upward comparisons made through social media had a terrible impact on women's mood and could be particularly harmful for their mental and physical health.

Another study found that women who take and post selfies on social media felt more anxious and less physically attractive than those who did not post selfies in the control group. Interestingly, women continued to feel anxious even when they are given a chance to retake and retouch their selfies afterwards (Mills et al., 2018). The researchers explained that scrutinizing and editing their own images perhaps made the women give renewed attention to their perceived flaws which made them anxious.

Experts have pointed out that being unhappy with one's own body may lead to depression and eating disorders, especially in adolescent girls (Meier & Gray, 2014). Media reports claim that more people are requesting medical procedures to get their real-life images to resemble their app-perfected digital image, a phenomenon that is also referred to as "Snapchat dysmorphia" – a term coined by the cosmetic doctor Tijion Esho, founder of the Esho clinics in London and Newcastle (Hunt, 2015). In search of the perfect selfie, many want bigger eyes, enlarged lips, raised cheeks, and erasure of laugh lines and pores either by injecting fillers or through surgical procedures. Medical journals caution that such practices can trigger "body dysmorphic disorder" which is a "mental health condition where people become fixated on imagined defects in their appearance" (Hunt, 2015).

However, several scholars reject the usage of such a pathological lens to analyze selfie-related practices and hold alternative viewpoints both on selfies and selfie-takers. Let us explore such alternative perspectives in the section below.

Alternative perspectives: Why discipline young women for taking selfies?

Scholars who propose an alternative framework for understanding selfies highlight the need to go beyond focusing on a specific genre of selfies. After all, it has become second nature for many to click a selfie in an important moment of one's life and not necessarily only when one wants to attract attention to one's physical appearance. Rejecting reductive views of selfie-taking behaviors, some digital research scholars point out that selfies are not just about young girls posing with cell phones in hand but about photographs taken in a wide variety of contexts and moments including those in sports, politics, crime, or one's own illness. Hence, Senft and Baym argue that the language afforded by "19th-century psychoanalysis" may not be adequate to analyze these selfies and the motivations of selfie-takers (p. 1590).

Then again, women and people at the margins of society are more socially policed for taking and posting selfies than others (Senft & Baym, 2015). Annie Burns, a selfie researcher in the United Kingdom, observes that criticism of selfies and selfie-takers reflects contemporary anxieties relating to the behavior of young women and aims at ensuring they comply with social norms. While portraying female selfie-takers as self-obsessed and vain people with an exaggerated concern for one's own appearance, popular discourse encourages disciplining of women's behavior online and justifies the expression of misogynistic beliefs (Burns, 2015). It also regulates the expression of female sexuality online even as it portrays frequent selfie-takers as attention-deprived thereby reinforcing patriarchal structures and strictures. Burns (2015) argues:

> Alongside this stigmatizing of women's selfies exists the expectation of self-regulation, the urging of women to exercise restraint in order to get "lifelong respect" rather than "instant gratification." By taking photographs that are read as indicating her own impurity, the female selfie taker is held as responsible for both the viewer's disdain and for her own marginalization. (p. 1724)

Thus, women are advised to limit the number of selfies they take and post on social media forums even as prescriptions on how to take selfies that reflect socially acceptable femininity are also given (Burns, 2015). In the following section, we seek to explore selfies that go beyond what is considered normative and socially acceptable.

Alternative selfies

Domestic violence survivor selfie: Taking a stand

Several domestic violence survivors have posted selfies including graphic photographs of their bruised faces and injured bodies on social media forums. For instance, Angela Brower, a 37-year-old American woman, posted selfies of her severely battered face on Facebook in the year 2014 with the caption "Does this look like love to anyone of you?" She documented her recovery journey on Facebook as she "underwent surgery to remove bone fragments from her face and to place a metal ring around her eye to stop it from collapsing" (Jeltsen, 2014). In a media interview, she said she wanted to spread awareness about domestic abuse so women can get out of bad situations before they get even worse.

Sadly, such domestic violence survivor selfies are a growing phenomenon. Mark Wood and his colleagues at the University of Melbourne argue that the attention that graphic and gruesome selfies of domestic violence survivors get online in terms of views, likes, comments, and shares on social media forums illustrates a distinct form of "online informal justice" that they term "viral justice." Domestic violence survivors' posts "may function not only to name and shame perpetrators, but also to document evidence, garner personal recognition or support and increase the visibility of the harm" (Wood et al., 2019, p. 377).

However, Mark Wood and his fellow researchers also point out that apart from acknowledging the affordances offered by social media, it is also important to recognize other factors that operate in such a context. For instance, the domestic violence survivor loses control over her selfie and her narrative the moment she posts it on a social media platform and it travels through multiple unknown networks drawing varied responses from users. One may also witness "keyboard activism" in such situations where users feel they have done their part to fight domestic violence by liking, commenting, and sharing the selfie with their own online network and do little else. Further, viral selfies of domestic violence survivors may lead to a focus on individual cases that are perceived as aberrant while domestic violence is commonplace and systemic and needs deep sociocultural and attitudinal change (Wood et al., 2019).

Moreover, we also need to keep in mind the conditions of those who do not have access to social media and cannot voice their opinions online. We also need to understand the dilemmas of those who have access to social media but cannot imagine posting their domestic violence stories on public platforms due to dangers to their lives and accompanying social ostracization, especially in patriarchal societies that normalize such violence.

Rape survivor selfies: Project Unbreakable

Browsing through the images posted on the Project Unbreakable blog on Tumblr can be an overwhelming experience (projectunbreakable.tumblr. com). On this blog, one can find images of thousands of rape and sexual abuse survivors posted in selfie format with the person holding a placard with handwritten text on it. The text usually comprises words spoken by the rapist during the assault.

For instance, of the placards reads "You f***ing whore, don't lie you wanted it – Abuser #2." Yet another placard reads "'Ssshhh…you'll learn to like it' – my father (9-11 years old). I am 15 now. I have never confronted anyone about it." In some of these images, one can see the face while others show the upper body. In some images, one can only see the hands holding the placard.

The project was founded in 2009 by then photography student Grace Brown after she was gravely affected listening to a friend's account of sexual abuse and wanted to do something about it (Ferreday, 2017). The blog declares the aim of the project as giving "voice to survivors of sexual assault, domestic violence and child abuse."

Debra Ferreday (2017) in her chapter titled "Like a Stone in Your Stomach: Articulating the Unspeakable in Rape Victim-Survivors' Activist Selfies" explains:

> The viral and proliferating nature of selfie culture potentially creates, then, a sense of community, of safety in numbers, which makes it possible for survivors to waive the anonymity (and hence the isolation) that is the sole protection afforded them by the neo-liberal state. (p. 134)

Then again, one should not assume that digital spaces are necessarily safe for women. Those who express strong opinions online that run counter to what is considered socially normative are trolled relentlessly and even receive rape threats at times (Ferreday, 2017).

Illness selfie: Spreading awareness

People may take selfies when they are sick and post them on social media platforms. Amongst such selfies, "autopathographic" selfies include those that offer a "first-person-perspective on experiences of illness or hospitalization" (Tembeck, 2016, p.1). Autopathography is a subgenre of autobiography where the word "bios" is replaced with the word "pathos" as images and narratives in this field portray one's own experience with something traumatic such as illness or an accident. Tamar Tembeck, a researcher at McGill University in Canada identifies three primary types of autopathographic selfies: diagnostic selfies, cautionary selfies, and treatment impact selfies. However, we cannot put these categories in watertight compartments as there are bound to be overlaps and all of them help to educate people about various aspects of an ailment.

The case of Stacey Yepes, a 49-year-old Canadian woman, comprises an excellent example of a diagnostic selfie as doctors diagnosed her ailment from a selfie video that she had recorded (Tembeck, 2016). Yepes had visited a hospital to report what appeared to her to be signs of a stroke but the doctors dismissed the possibility as her tests had been clear (CBC News, 2014). However, two days later, she left a numbing sensation on the left side of her face and had trouble speaking or smiling while she was driving. She pulled over to the side of the road and recorded a selfie-video of her face which helped doctors realize that she was indeed having a mini-stroke (CBC News, 2014). Later, Yepes also posted the video on YouTube to educate others about the signs of a stroke.

People also take selfies to caution others about the possible consequences of their actions. For instance, one can find selfies on social media of wounds and fungal infections caused by visits to unhygienic hair and nail salons. People with terminal ailments such as cancer may post treatment-impact selfies to highlight the impact of chemotherapy or a particular treatment regimen. If you key the words "chemotherapy selfie" on the Internet, you will see how many cancer patients have documented their journeys using selfies. Time lapse videos showing how chemotherapy ravages the human body and causes hair loss in people have been documented by many cancer patients.

Armpit hair selfie: Redefining feminine beauty

In the year 2014, a trend started in the United States that involved celebrities and ordinary women posting selfies of colored armpit hair on social media forums. It spread to different parts of the world. In China, a group of women held an armpit hair competition for two consecutive years. In the year 2015, prizes were announced for those with the most "characteristic and beautiful and confident" online display of armpit hair (House, 2015). The competition was aimed at resisting social norms that view armpit hair in women as disgusting.

Rebecca Tuhus-Dubrow (2019) points out the difference between feminist rejection of bras, stilettos, and even razors in the 1960s and 1970s and the current online displays of armpit hair. She explains:

> Today's renewed enthusiasm for female hirsuteness comes with a distinctly 21st-century twist. Unshaven women in 2019 often meet other criteria for traditional feminine beauty – they have sculpted eyebrows, wear lipstick or sexy lingerie – while proudly displaying their armpit hair. If the ethos of the 70s was a refusal to spend time and effort on cosmetics, the more common approach today is for women to curate different elements of their appearance, remaining conventionally attractive while deploying body hair as a feminist f***-you: half-statement, half-ornament. (Tuhus-Dubrow, 2019)

Since selfies of women with armpit hair are highly "social-mediagenic," they go viral in no time (Tuhus-Dubrow, 2019). However, it must be remembered that it takes courage to post pictures of oneself with armpit hair on the Internet as such visuals get rude and nasty comments.

Most women continue to internalize the ideal that they need to have shaved arms and legs as any visible hair on their limbs would raise eyebrows at least in public spaces. In fact, a woman with hair on her arms and legs is considered such an unforgivable sight that even razor advertisements for women on television show models shaving perfectly hairless legs (Tuhus-Dubrow, 2019). While the armpit hair selfies may not have changed such ideals instantaneously, they have definitely started a conversation on what comprises feminine beauty and whether we should have any fixed standards about them and by whom.

Nude selfie: Look at my body

Katrin Tiidenberg, a social studies researcher, examined how "not safe for work" (NFSW) selfie-bloggers on Tumblr used their images to promote what they considered a "body-positive environment" that resists normative prescriptions on what a beautiful body should look like. The people Tiidenberg interviewed said they found the posting of headless, nude, and semi-nude images therapeutic as it made them feel "like a sexual, gendered, embodied person, rather than, for example just a mother, a PTA member or an employee." Apart from the selfies helping them address body image issues, they claimed that the activity also increased their life satisfaction as it helped in "getting one's sexy back" (Tiidenberg, 2014).

In a similar study, Matt Hart, a researcher at Western Sydney University, interviewed 25 young men and women who posted nude selfies on their

Tumblr blogs to identify possible benefits from such a practice and found that they felt "empowered, free, and excited or aroused" (p. 11). These young men and women said they did not expect people unfamiliar with selfie-blogging to understand why they posted such selfies. While a young woman claimed she posted nudes because she has "always lived a rebellious life," an 18-year-old White man said he felt great when people commented positively on his pictures as he did not consider himself particularly attractive.

Another 19-year-old said she found posting nude selfies on Tumblr a good way to highlight her transgendered identity which she could not disclose to her own family. The study also illuminated the intensity of the respondents' involvement in taking selfies even as they lost track of time clicking pictures, editing them and posting them online with the goal of finding "a connection to their bodies" that they had not found elsewhere (Hart, 2017, p. 311).

These studies show how the practice of taking selfies meets different needs and has different motivations for different people. In fact, individuals belonging to the LGBT community were drawn towards representing themselves online before heterosexual men and women as online spaces gave them relatively more freedom to represent themselves than the offline world (Eler, 2019). A gender-queer individual in Toronto pointed out that selfies can be viewed as "acts of resistance" that disrupt what is considered normative in the mainstream media thereby giving individuals the agency to define their own standard of beauty, gender, and sexuality (Eler, 2019).

Stephen Barnard, an American sociologist, is critical of the empowering trope used to describe some selfie-taking activities. He argues that "the intended messages about health, body positivity, and self(ie)-empowerment are being undermined by the hegemony of feminine, body-focused selfies and the stubbornness of the male gaze" (p. 78). He also points out that people generally use selfies to express themselves at a personal level and hence such acts cannot be viewed as political acts or as making any contribution to the feminist movement. However, it needs to be mentioned here that Barnard probably fails to understand that the nature of activism is changing today. While the power of collective offline action remains critical for change, one cannot underestimate the power of online personal expression either.

Selfies: A different visual language

Most people today fall into two opposing camps in terms of their views on selfies. While one camp views selfies as an empowering and democratizing project, the other one views it as representing all that is wrong with this world (Shah, 2015). Such overwhelming binaries, in turn, obfuscate the nuanced contexts in which selfies are taken, shared, and viewed. Whether a selfie is empowering or not would depend on the context in which it was taken, by whom, and for what purpose. Moreover, it may not subscribe to the empowering/disempowering binary at all. In such a complex scenario, digital culture scholars highlight how this misleading rhetoric about all selfies being either a source of empowerment or disempowerment continues to persist (Senft & Baym, 2015).

Instead, it is important for us to acknowledge that selfies comprise a new visual language that cannot be reduced to a label based on one's own beliefs, biases, and prejudice. Instead, one should strive to understand the sociocultural and personal context in which the selfie is taken. For instance, interviews with people living in the urban slums of Brazil, who live in constant fear of powerful drug lords, showed that their selfie-taking habits had nothing to do with narcissism and attention seeking at all. Instead, they took selfies to express their emotions including anger and frustration, and to communicate with people, as they did not know how to read or write (Nemer & Freeman, 2015, p. 1837).

In a different context, when young people started taking selfies at funerals in the United States, allegations of self-obsession ran rife. Jason Feifer, the American journalist who created the viral Tumblr blog on young men and women taking funeral selfies, argued that such selfies do not necessarily highlight self-centeredness among millennials:

> When a teen tweets out a funeral selfie, their friends don't castigate them. They understand that their friend, in their own way, is expressing an emotion they may not have words for. It's a visual language that older people – even those like me, in their 30s – simply don't speak.
>
> (Feifer, 2012)

Selfie researchers have expressed similar viewpoints. James Meese (2015) and his team of researchers at the University of Melbourne examined funeral selfies on Instagram, a platform where posting selfies is "an established vernacular practice" and found that while funeral selfies may appear narcissistic and even carry insensitive hashtags at times, they are often about a person trying to visually communicate his or her presence at a funeral and the emotional state at that time with no intention to trivialize the ceremony or the deceased.

Instead, the practice of taking funeral selfies reflects a shift in people's attitudes towards taking photographs (Meese et al., 2015). After digital cameras became popular, people started taking pictures more often to visually communicate about what they were doing in a particular moment than for the purpose of preserving memories for posterity, which was the main purpose of taking photographs in a pre-digital era.

Further, one should not assume that people who use the new visual language of selfies do not care about privacy at all. They probably see privacy as more nuanced than previous generations did (Walsh & Baker, 2016). Selfie-takers continually define what privacy means to them even as they decide which aspects of their lives to reveal and which to conceal. Of course, people have been deciding which aspects of themselves to show and which to hide right from the beginning but what makes things different today is the ease of manipulation and the degree of control offered by digital devices.

In view of the changes introduced by our digital practices, Sarah Michelle Ford, a sociologist at the University of Massachusetts, points out that we need to reconceptualize the public–private distinction and view it as a continuum rather than as dichotomous realms. Ford argues that "nothing is ever truly public or truly private" but we strive "to give more or less access to information about ourselves based on what we feel to be situationally appropriate" (Ford, 2011, p. 560).

The spread of the new visual language of selfies has implications for corporations as well since they introduce new challenges for brand management and customer engagement. Consumers may create new meanings for brands based on the nature of selfies they take and post thereby disrupting what is perceived as the traditional image of a brand (Rokka & Canniford, 2016). For instance, a well-known five-star hotel in Dubai formally requested its guests to stop taking bathroom selfies in the hotel's lavish facilities and posting them on social media platforms as they did not want to see their geolocation "on photos of girls in semi-naked and erotic poses" (Saner, 2017). Well, brands need to find a way to integrate heterogenous selfie practices that presumably challenge their identity.

Marketers also need to understand the cultural nuances embedded in selfies. For instance, an analysis of selfies posted on Twitter in the United Kingdom and those on Sina Weibo in China showed that Chinese selfies often present an "ideal self" and usually do not disclose the location (Ma et al., 2017). Meanwhile, UK selfies on Twitter often disclosed locations and commonly focused on the selfie-taker's sex appeal. Furthermore, marketers will miss out on a lot of rich data if they view the selfie merely as a narcissistic tool. They need to understand the myriad and complex reasons why people take and post selfies on social media.

Finally, focusing on selfie-taking practices on mainstream social media platforms such as Facebook, Twitter, and Instagram alone will lead to all of us missing out on the more engaged and invested performances of identity in pseudonymous and anonymous online environments. A person may post a specific type of selfie on Facebook and a completely different one on Reddit or Tumblr. Trying to find a universal explanation for people's selfie-related practices is a futile affair (Tiidenberg, 2018). Attaching a fixed label to people's selfie-related practices will only hide the complexities of human nature instead of illuminating them. Instead, we need to acknowledge, understand, and embrace the heterogeneity of purposes for which selfies are taken, posted, shared, viewed, and commented upon.

References

Bansal, A., Garg, C., Pakhare, A., & Gupta, S. (2018). Selfies: A boon or bane? *Journal of Family Medicine & Primary Care, 7*(4), 828–831.

Barnard, S. R. (2016). Spectacles of self(ie) empowerment? Networked individualism and the logic of the (post)feminist selfie. *Communication and Information Technologies Annual, 11,* 63–88. doi: 10.1108/S2050-206020160000011014

Burns, A. (2015). Self(ie)-discipline: Social regulation as enacted through the discussion of photographic practice. *International Journal of Communication, 9,* 1716–1733.

Döring, N., Reifl, A., & Poeschl, S. (2016). How gender-stereotypical are selfies? A content analysis and comparison with magazine adverts. *Computers in Human Behavior, 55,* 955–962.

Eager, T., & Dann, S. (2016). Classifying the narrated #selfie: Genre typing human-branding activity. *European Journal of Marketing, 50*(9/10), 1835–1857.

Eler, A. (2019, August 18). *There's a lot more to a selfie than meets the eye.* Retrieved from https://www.salon.com/2019/08/18/theres-a-lot-more-to-a-selfie-than-meets-the-eye/

Fardouly, J., Pinkus, R. T., & Vartanian, L. R. (2017). The impact of appearance comparisons made through social media, traditional media, and in person in women's everyday lives. *Body Image, 20,* 31–39.

Feifer, J. (2013, December 11). Obama's funeral selfie is a fitting end to my Tumblr – Selfies at Funerals. *The Guardian.* Retrieved from https://www.theguardian.com/commentisfree/2013/dec/11/obama-funeral-selfie-tumblr-mandela-teens

Ferreday, D. (2017). Like a stone in your stomach: Articulating the unspeakable in rape victim-survivors. In A. Kuntsman (Ed.), *Selfie Citizenship.* Manchester, UK: Palgrave Macmillan.

Ford, S. M. (2011). Reconceptualizing the public/private distinction in the age of information technology. *Information, Communication & Society, 14*(4), 550–567. doi: 10.1080/1369118X.2011.562220

Fox, J., & Rooney, M. C. (2015). The dark triad and trait self-objectification as predictors of men's use and self-presentation behaviors on social networking sites. *Personality and Individual Differences, 76,* 161–165. doi: 10.1016/j.paid.2014.12.017

Garber, M. (2014, October 1). The end of the selfie hype cycle. *The Atlantic.* Retrieved from http://www.theatlantic.com/technology/archive/2014/10/selfies-are-boring-nowand-thats-why-theyre-finally-interesting/381001/

Hart, M. (2017). Being naked on the internet: Young people's selfies as intimate edgework, *Journal of Youth Studies*, *20*(3), 301–315. doi: 10.1080/13676261. 2016.1212164

House, L. (2015, June 10). Armpit hair, don't care! Chinese women flood social media with hairy underarm selfies to prove they don't need to be hairless to be beautiful. *Daily Mail*. Retrieved from dailymail.co.uk/femail/article-3117696/A rmpit-hair-don-t-care-Chinese-women-flood-social-media-hairy-underarm-selfi es-prove-beautiful.html

Hunt, E. (2019, January 23). Faking it: How selfie dysmorphia is driving people to seek surgery. *The Guardian*. Retrieved from https://www.theguardian.com/ lifeandstyle/2019/jan/23/faking-it-how-selfie-dysmorphia-is-driving-people-to -seek-surgery

IANS. (2016, June 23). How selfie in Ganga led to the death of 7 students. https:/ /www.indiatoday.in/india/story/how-selfie-in-ganga-led-to-the-death-of-7-stude nts-15776-2016-06-23

Jeltsen, M. (2014). Woman posts domestic violence selfies to Facebook. *Huffington Post*. Retrieved from https://www.huffingtonpost.in/entry/domestic-violence_

Lebowitz, S. (2011). Here's what people really think when you make a 'duck face' in your selfie. *Business Insider*. Retrieved from https://www.businessinsider.com /what-duck-face-reveals-about-your-personality-2016-7?IR=T

Liddy, M. (2013). This photo, posted on ABC online, is the world's first known 'selfie'. *Australian Broadcasting Cooperation News*. Retrieved https://www.abc .net.au/news/2013-11-19/this-photo-is-worlds-first-selfie/5102568

Ma, J. W., Yang, Y., & Wilson, J. A. J. (2017). A window to the ideal self: A study of UK Twitter and Chinese Sina Weiboselfie-takers and the implications for marketers. *Journal of Business Research*, *74*, 139–142.

Maddox, J. (2017). "Guns don't kill people … Selfies do": Rethinking narcissism as exhibitionism in selfie-related deaths. *Critical Studies in Media Communication*, *34*(3), 193–205. doi: 10.1080/15295036.2016.1268698

Meese, J., Gibbs, M., Carter, M., Arnold, M., Nansen, B., & Kohn, T. (2015). Selfies at funerals: Mourning and presencing on social media platforms. *International Journal of Communication*, *9*, 1818–1831.

Meier, E. P., & Gray, J. (2014). Facebook photo activity associated with body image disturbance in adolescent girls. *Cyberpsychology, Behavior and Social Networking*, *17*, 199–206. doi: 10.1089/cyber.2013.0305

Mills, J. S., Mustoa, S., Williams, L., & Tiggemann, M. (2018). "Selfie" harm: Effects on mood and body image in young women. *Body Image*, *27*, 86–92.

Murray, D. C. (2020). Selfie consumerism in a narcissistic age. *Consumption Markets & Culture*, *23*(1), 21–43. doi: 10.1080/10253866.2018.1467318

Nemeri, D., & Freeman, G. (2015). Empowering the marginalized: Rethinking selfies in the slums of Brazil. *International Journal of Communication*, *9*, 1832–1847.

Rokka, J., & Canniford, R. (2016). Heterotopian selfies: How social media destabilizes brand assemblages. *European Journal of Marketing*, *50*(9/10), 1789–1813.

Saner, E. (2017, January 24). Are you finished in there yet? How the bathroom selfie became so huge. *The Guardian*. Retrieved from https://www.theguardian.c

om/media/shortcuts/2017/jan/24/finished-in-there-yet-how-bathroom-selfie-be
came-huge

'Selfie', coined on ABC Online in 2002, beats 'twerk' to be named as Oxford's 2013 word of the year 19 Nov 2013, ABC News, 2013. https://www.abc.net.au/news /2013-11-19/selfie-beats-twerk-as-word-of-the-year/5102154

Selfiecity. (2014). Retrieved from http://selfiecity.net/

Senft, T., & Baym, N. (2015). What does the selfie say? Investigating a global phenomenon. *International Journal of Communication, 9*. Retrieved from http:/ /ijoc.org/index.php/ijoc/article/view/4067/1387

Shah, N. (2015, April 25). The selfie and the slut: Bodies, technology and public shame. *Economic & Political Weekly, 1*(17), 86–93.

Stroke diagnosis made through woman's selfie video (2014, June 16). *CBC News*. Retrieved from https://www.cbc.ca/news/health/stroke-diagnosis-made-through -woman-s-selfie-video-1.2677550

Tembeck, T. (2016). Selfies of ill health: Online autopathographic photography and the dramaturgy of the everyday. *Social Media + Society, 2*(1), 1–11.

Tiidenberg, K. (2014). Bringing sexy back: Reclaiming the body aesthetic via self-shooting. *Cyberpsychology: Journal of Psychosocial Research on Cyberspace, 8*(1). Retrieved from http://cyberpsychology.eu/view.php?cisloclanku=201 4021701&article=3

Tiidenberg, K. (2018). *Selfies: Why we love (and hate) them.* [Series: Society Now] Bingley: Emerald Publishing.

Tuhus-Dubrow, R. (2019). The new feminist armpit hair revolution: half-statement, half-ornament. *The Guardian*. Retrieved from https://www.theguardian.com/ lifeandstyle/2019/jun/24/feminist-armpit-hair-revolution-half-statement-half-ornament

Walsh, M. J., & Baker, S. A. (2016). The selfie and the transformation of the public–private distinction, *Information, Communication & Society.* doi: 10.1080/1369118X.2016.1220969

Wood, M., Rose, E., & Thompson, C. (2019). Viral justice? Online justice seeking, intimate partner violence and affective contagion. *Theoretical Criminology, 23*(3), 375–393.

2 "Send me a sexy picture"

Love, intimacy, and infidelity in the digital era

In the year 2000, two 14-year-olds, Joanna and Tristan, who lived on opposite coasts of the United States, started chatting online. After chatting on the Internet for 9 years, they decided to meet in Seattle. Despite interacting online for so many years, they felt nervous before seeing each other for the first time at Seattle airport. Their first offline meeting led to many realizations. For instance, Tristan realized he was an inch shorter than Joanna. While he had really enjoyed Joanna's laughs and the "HaHa" that followed his funny messages, he discovered that he really loved her smile. Joanna also found out that she loved the way Tristan smelled. Eight years after their first real-life meeting in Seattle, the two got married in New York in 2017 (Mallozzi, 2017).

Joanna and Tristan's story could be called the "fairy tale" of online relationships. Such stories are rare as most online interactions do not end this way. Moreover, not everyone desires such an ending. Much has changed in contemporary dating cultures even as dating sites have metamorphosed into mobile apps with many young users showing a preference for brief messages and instant gratification. Long, romantic emails seem to have become a relic of the past. Instead, location-based dating apps such as Tinder ensure that people can meet offline within minutes of finding each other on the app.

Massive changes in the way people express both love and lust have given rise to multiple dilemmas. For instance, will people fall in and out of love in ways that are different from before? Will the rise of "hook up culture" signal the end of emotional intimacy in dating? How will contemporary digital cultures redefine romantic commitment? Will more people cheat on each other since it is much easier to do so today than ever before? There are no shortcut answers to these complex questions. To arrive at some sort of understanding of where these questions come from and what their possible answers could be, we need to explore contemporary forms of dating, intimacy, and infidelity with an open mind.

This chapter will start with a discussion of mobile dating with a special focus on Tinder, the world's most popular dating app (Jansen, 2020). It will then explore the nature and implications of sexting, a widely popular form of intimate communication today. We will then examine varied digital manifestations of infidelity before we conclude the chapter with a look at future possibilities.

Tinder and "hook ups": Your place, mine, or somewhere else

Before we begin discussing mobile dating apps, let us explore what "hooking up" really means today. The Cambridge English Dictionary defines "hook up" as starting "a romantic or sexual relationship with someone." However, according to the Urban Dictionary, which is a crowdsourced online dictionary for slangs and phrase, "hook up" refers to the following:

> To have any form of intimacy with a member of the preferred sex that you don't consider a significant other. Usually, when said by modern youth it means to make out, and when said by people between the ages of 20 and 35 it generally means to have sex, and if a very old person says it, it probably means to simply spend time with somebody.

Some users have compared mobile dating to online shopping with the exception being that you are ordering a person after checking out their picture online instead of an item or thing (Sales, 2015).

Dating apps today are more focused on visuals than dating websites that were previously popular. For instance, on Tinder, people swipe right to show they like the person, or left when they are not interested in that person primarily by looking at their photographs. One of the principles that Tinder is based on is that people do not really show interest in someone they meet at a gathering based on detailed information about their hobbies and interests. Instead they usually reach out based on the cues they get by simply looking at another person (Bilton, 2014). In fact, the first thing we notice about a person when we see them and before we have had a chance to talk to them is how they look.

Since Tinder profiles offer limited information and decisions are based on people's photographs, one may assume that the most physically attractive people would automatically get the maximum number of matches on Tinder. However, reality presents a more nuanced picture. Dating experts at Tinder believe people try to deduce potential compatibility not just on a physical level but on a social level as well (Bilton, 2014). For instance, how a person poses for a picture, what he or she is wearing, where the photograph was taken, etc., give out multiple cues about the person and what he or she might be like.

In fact, a study conducted by Tinder showed that women almost always swiped left when shown pictures of male models with chiselled faces as they assumed these men would be too self-obsessed and unkind. Although men generally swipe right more often than women, even they don't always base their decisions on anatomy alone (Bilton, 2014). Moreover, different people have different notions of beauty and attractiveness.

While media reports present Tinder as merely a "hook up app," academic research highlights associated complexities. Researchers in the Netherlands and Belgium identified six motivations amongst young adults who use Tinder including love, casual sex, ease of communication, self-worth, validation, thrill of excitement and trendiness, which varied according to age and gender (Sumter et al., 2017). Also, men were more likely to report casual sex as their motivation for using Tinder than women. Similarly, men were also more likely to use Tinder for the thrill of it than women.

The study showed that while casual sex is an important reason why people use Tinder, it's not the only one. People feel good when others show interest in them. They feel validated. Moreover, the study also found that the love motivation to use Tinder was stronger than the casual sex motivation as many were seeking relationships on it. Further, both love and casual sex motivations were positively related with age (Sumter et al., 2017).

Since so many people are looking for partners online, impression management on dating apps and sites becomes critical for them. Previous research shows that while women are strategic about their appearance and may lie about their weight online, men tend to lie about their relationship status (Ranzini & Lutz, 2017). In the case of Tinder, scholars have found that people who are seeking relationships on Tinder are more likely to be authentic in their self-representation than those who are seeking sex and self-validation. People with high self-esteem are likely to be less deceptive in their self-presentation on Tinder (Ranzini & Lutz, 2017).

Sherry Turkle, an MIT professor, argues that while technology makes romance more efficient, it takes away the very essence of it:

> Human relationships are rich, messy, and demanding. When we clean them up with technology, *we move from conversation to the efficiencies of mere connection* [sic]. (Turkle, 2015, p. 21)

For instance, a couple may be texting each other the entire day and end up not having said anything meaningful to each other. Most of the exchanges between young people may be texts that merely ask mundane questions such as "What's up?" or "Where are you?" and rarely delving into deeper conversations (Turkle, 2011). Of course, mundane questions have their place in any relationship but making them the mainstay may not be desirable.

Digital technology also offers people infinite choice in partners rendering it difficult to stick to one (Turkle, 2015). If one is unhappy with their current partner, another person is just a swipe or click away. Infinite choice may keep a person permanently engaged in chasing the illusive right one. With so many dating apps available today, it is easy to meet a high number of potential partners in a short amount of time. What is tough is investing the time and effort to really get to know someone when there are so many others lurking on our cell phones ("Internet dating," 2015). In fact, it is not uncommon today for someone to continue swiping on Tinder when they are already on a date with one person just to check out the dating scene in that area.

Digital technology has not only changed how we find love and sex, but also how we get out of a relationship. It has made forgetting and moving on more complicated than before. For instance, it is easy to keep revisiting an ex's profile on Facebook or other social media platforms. Facebook gives many former couples awkward moments when it reminds them of friendship anniversaries or shows a picture of a former partner's current romantic interest in the newsfeed.

Of course, digital technology also offers many advantages. Apps make it easier to "ignore being ignored" (Turkle, 2015, p. 179). For instance, no one knows when they have been rejected or swiped left on Tinder. They only get to know when they swipe right and the other person also swipes right creating a match. Thus, one can reject and be rejected by hundreds of potential partners without anyone getting to know. It saves everyone many awkward and embarrassing moments.

But what really happens when "hook up" culture collides with "Indian" cultural sensibilities? In India, dating apps including Tinder, Bumble, TrulyMadly, OkCupid and Happn have gained popularity. Although metros and big cities are big markets for such dating apps, young men and women from Tier II cities such as Indore, Ahmedabad, Lucknow, Bhopal, Ranchi, Rajkot and Vadodara are also showing interest (Jha, 2019).

While India's mofussil towns and rural areas don't seem to have opened up to dating app culture, a gay dating and social networking app, Blued India, claims that 20–30% of its user base comes from small towns. The app allows customization in seven Indian languages including Hindi, Malayalam, Tamil, Telugu, Kannada, Marathi, and Punjabi (Jha, 2019). Such diversification reflects the growing demand for dating apps in India. Apart from greater access to digital technology, the popularity of dating apps in India amongst young people could be a culmination of changing attitudes toward romantic relationships, financial independence, a desire to be viewed as "modern" by their peers and an eagerness to be part of a worldwide cultural trend (Jha, 2019).

Although dating apps are becoming popular in India, gender plays a big role in determining the nature of one's experience on them. For instance, young Indian women who use dating apps have to negotiate sociocultural anxieties at multiple levels. They not only have to ensure that their presence on a dating app remains hidden from their families and relatives, they also have to prepare themselves to deal with the misogyny and sexist behavior that many Indian men display on these dating apps and the dates that follow (Yashaswi, 2020).

Female users of dating apps report that it is difficult for many Indian men to respect a woman who is upfront about her sexual desires (Yashaswi, 2020). There have been cases of men stalking women on social media platforms after they were rejected on a dating app and cases of assault during dates set up using an app. Since dating apps are associated with multiple anxieties in Indian society, "'casual' sex is often bereft of the breezy nonchalance that the term implies, even though it is just a swipe away" (Yashaswi, 2020). Complaints of harassment on dating apps have led to the rise of female-centric apps such as Bumble and Gleeden. We will now explore sexting, an outcome of present-day mobile dating practices.

Sexting: Nudes, semi-nudes, and other pictures

Why do people sext?

Sexting refers to "sending or posting of sexually suggestive text messages and images, including nude or semi-nude photographs, via mobiles or over the Internet" (Cooper et al., 2016, p. 707). Surveys indicate sexting predominantly occurs among young people who know one another as friends, acquaintances, or current or potential romantic partners (Setty, 2019).

While some may use sexting as an important way to keep a long-distance relationship alive, others may consider it just as another form of digital flirting. Overall, young people engage in sexting for primarily four reasons: To flirt or gain attention of someone they are interested in; to experiment with one's sexuality in the adolescent phase; as part of a consensual relationship, and finally, due to pressure from a partner or friend (Cooper et al., 2016).

Boys are more likely to pressure a partner to sext than girls (Kernsmith et al., 2018). More teen girls than boys tend to *send* sexual images, according to a survey conducted in the United States and the pattern continues into young adulthood as well (Chalfen, 2009). Young men and teenage boys may also demand sexual images from women due to peer pressure on them. Karen Cooper and her fellow researchers elaborate on this type of behavior:

Boys in particular may seek to illustrate to their ability to chat to girls and to negotiate access to seeing their bodies. This includes tagging, sending and sharing pictures of girls' bodies, particularly their breasts, in order to prove their sexual activity and to gain status among their peers. (Cooper et al., 2016, p. 710)

Apart from getting coerced to engage in sexting, women may also send pictures due to social pressure which expects them to have the ability to woo men with their sex appeal alone. The sexualization of women in the media may lead to girls objectifying themselves early in life. They may start believing that they are objects meant to be looked at and evaluated by others (APA, 2007).

Additionally, many people who send sexual images do not realize that digital images are permanent in nature and can be infinitely circulated amongst people without their consent, making them highly risky records of intimate moments. Research indicates that it is primarily women and children who are victims of such non-consensual distribution of sexual imagery (Powell, 2010). The non-consensual distribution of sexual images often following a break-up is called "revenge porn" in popular parlance (Cooper et al., 2016, p. 711). The images may have been taken with consent but a former partner may distribute them among friends or post them online as an act of revenge. He or she may also resort to threats and blackmail pertaining to the images after the relationship is over and can cause a lot of harm in the process.

In the case of India, research shows that more Indians have *received* sexts than *sent* them, implying that a small number of senders probably distribute to a larger audience here (Klettke et al., 2018). When intimate images of a woman are leaked online in a patriarchal society like India, grave consequences follow. For instance, most Indians are aware of the infamous "DPS MMS scandal" which rocked the country in 2004 when a video of two school students engaging in sexual act was leaked online. The boy had recorded the video of the girl performing a sexual act and circulated it amongst his friends (PTI, 2004). The leaking of the video led to many Indians questioning why the girl did it and why she let him film it even as very few asked if the girl had given him permission to share the video in the first place (Padte, 2015). Little seems to have changed today in terms of mind-sets of people in Indian society and their victim-blaming attitudes.

Sexting experiences vary with gender

Sexting is a gendered experience. While women are shamed for sexting, many men gain "social capital" through it (Setty, 2019). The responsibility of managing the sexting habits of young men is often placed on women. It is women who are held responsible when a man distributes their sexual images to an unintended audience without their consent.

In today's youth cultures, young women are often caught in a dilemma about sexting. A young woman risks being considered frigid and not doing enough to maintain the sexual interest of her partner if she does not engage in sexting. On the other hand, she risks being socially shamed if she does (Setty, 2019).

Interviews with youth in the United States reveal that while young women who engaged in sexting were often viewed as "easy" and "slutty," men who did so were considered "cool" and "confident" (Setty, 2019). Women engaging in sexting were also considered to have low self-esteem while men doing the same were considered normal. In fact, young men pressurizing women to send sexual imagery or violating their privacy by sharing them without their consent was dismissed as "boys being boys" (Setty, 2019). Meanwhile, young women internalized the blame when things went wrong and berated themselves for participating in sexting instead of holding the men responsible for breaching their trust (Setty, 2019).

The interviews also revealed that while viewing sexts was considered normal and acceptable among young men, men sending their own nude images were viewed as "funny" and "comical" by others (Setty, 2020). Interestingly, men who did not engage in viewing or sending sexual images at the personal level, claimed to enjoy it when they discussed sexting in groups to show their adherence to hegemonic definitions of masculinity that views macho-ness positively. Furthermore, when a nude image of a young man was leaked to an unintended audience, other men expected him to not get affected emotionally and just take it in their stride. Such social and peer expectations prevented those young men who were emotionally traumatized from the event to articulate their feelings (Setty, 2020).

Research indicates women get more distressed revisiting and recounting a time when they were coerced into sexting than what they felt during the event. In fact, the level of distrust reportedly increased with time for many women who were coerced into sexting than decrease (Drouin et al., 2015).

Contextualizing sexting practices:

News reports primarily focus on sensational cases of sexting gone wrong. Such event-based reports rarely historicize the practice or contextualize it. While many news reports treat sexting as a new phenomenon, Richard Chalfen, a researcher at the Children's Hospital in Boston, points out that sexting could be viewed as "a new iteration of previous practices" (Chalfen, 2009, p. 259). Couples have always exchanged photographs of themselves with each other. Polaroid cameras and camcorders were also used by couples for similar purposes.

While such practices prevailed earlier, the Internet has made it easier to create, transfer, store, and leak personal sexual messages and imagery (Setty, 2019). In fact, Chalfen points out that young people today "live at the intersection of four different subcultures" including media culture, techno-culture, visual culture, and adolescent culture (p. 260). They are no longer just media consumers as they also produce media content. They are digital natives living in an intensely visual culture where people widely communicate through visual messages.

While attempting to understand sexting, one must make an attempt to understand the nuances involved and distinguish between the following sets of people and practices:

- those who consensually send images and those who are coerced into sending them
- those who take pictures and those who receive them
- those who choose to receive them and those who receive them by accident
- those who delete the pictures soon after receiving them and those who choose to retain them on their devices
- whether there are minors or adults involved in the process (Chalfen, 2009).

Most academic studies on adolescent texting highlight its risks and legal implications. However, there is a growing body of literature that addresses it as "normal" intimate communication in a digital world as opposed to the more common "deviance discourse" (Döring, 2014). For instance, Amy Adele Hasinoff (2012), a researcher at McGill University, suggests that sexting should be viewed as a form of "media production" which would consider potential benefits of the practice as well and not just frame it as a "technological, sexual and moral crisis" (p. 450).

She emphasizes that consensual intimate sexting should not be perceived as aberrant behavior although social norms usually frown upon women who express their sexual needs and desires. According to her, we should focus on raising awareness amongst young people about the need to respect another's person online privacy and discourage the tendency to view any teenager who engages in sexting as a criminal who deserves to be punished under child pornography laws. Instead, sexting among young adults may be viewed in the context of contemporary digital practices and the multiple ways in which teenagers explore their sexualities as a part of growing up (Kernsmith et al., 2018).

However, news media reports in India often warn people about the consequences of sexting with sensational headlines such as "Beware! Sexting can land you in trouble!" (Mumbai Mirror, 2017). But with extensive use of mobile phones in India and the ensuing COVID-19 pandemic, some news media outlets are approaching the issue from a different angle.

For example, an Indian news media report titled "Sexting Can Spice up Your Lockdown Days – Only if You are Careful" offered a list of precautions one could take while sexting including clear communication about one's boundaries, ensuring personal privacy by clicking faceless photos, and removing the metadata off one's files as it contains location, device, and timestamp details (Kapur, 2020). The report also counselled people who engage in sexting to be on the lookout for tell-tale signs that things would not end well such as a person sending unsolicited photos or repeatedly demanding them. Apart from the news media, schools can also play a vital role in preventing harmful fallouts of sexting.

Sex education at school can help adolescents cope

How can schools prevent harmful consequences of sexting? Let us take a recent example involving school-going adolescents. In the midst of a national lockdown imposed to contain the spread of the COVID-19 pandemic in India, news broke in May 2020 about the talk of gang rape on a private Instagram chat group called "bois locker room" (Matharu, 2020). The members of the group comprised teenage boys studying in class 10 and 11 at a top Delhi-based school. Apart from discussions about raping some of their classmates, the teenagers were also exchanging their nude photos and those of other underage women without their consent (Gupta, 2020).

The screenshots of the graphic chats were leaked on the Internet and they went viral in no time (Gupta, 2020). As the news spread, many expressed outrage on Twitter even as #boyslockerroom started trending on it as well. The nature of language used in the discussions unnerved a lot of people. People debated the case and what parents and schools could do about it. One wondered whether online discussions of sexual coercion could lead to real-life sexual violations.

While we do not have any definite answers to that question, it is worth mentioning a study here on coercive sexting practices by dating partners among high school and middle school students in the United States. In this study, a high degree of correlation was found between coercive sexting and more traditional forms of sexual coercion such as pressuring a date to have sex without a condom, insisting on sex when the partner refused to engage it, or threatening a partner into having sex, etc. (Kernsmith et al, 2018).

Keeping such situations in mind, schools must engage not just in educating students about the legal implications of sexting but also on the importance of consent in any form of intimacy. Such measures will help in preventing physical and psychological violence during dates between young boys and girls.

Legal scholars, Debarati Halder and K. Jaishankar, point out that suspending teenagers from schools for engaging in "revenge porn" or prosecuting them in traditional ways may not help. Instead, they advocate the use of "therapeutic jurisprudence" whereby the perpetrator teen is counselled to realize his mistake and made to engage in correctional works advised by a court. Meanwhile, the teen who has endured the harassment and violation of privacy should be given a platform to share their experience and seek redressal rights (Halder & Jaishankar, 2013).

Furthermore, sex education in schools should help teens develop a healthy sense of self. Such educational programs need to move beyond risk aversion and address contemporary practices related to adolescent sexuality in a digital era (Lloyd, 2020). Instead of merely recommending abstinence from sexting, which teenagers may not adhere, educational campaigns should counsel them on safe sexting practices that will help them take informed decisions and resist cyberbullying (Döring, 2014).

Apart from schools, parents also need to guide their children well in terms of navigating contemporary digital cultures and appropriate use of digital technology in interpersonal communication, especially in India, which is in the midst of tremendous social change following rapid urbanization and globalization (Brar et al., 2018). Teens and young adults should be counseled to be less impulsive and more cautious while using apps and social media platforms so they don't create a permanent record of a temporary feeling or moment.

Parents also need to ensure that they are counseling both their sons and daughters on safe sex. In case of daughters, it is important that parents accept female sexual desires as normal and healthy instead of labeling it as immoral or unnatural (Brar et al., 2018). In India, teens in rural area face great risk associated with sexting since they have less exposure to some of the negative consequences of sexting unlike their urban counterparts (Brar et al., 2018).

People should know their legal rights and know how to respond if someone threatens to leak their private messages or images. While all of us question why people take and send nude images, we often remain silent on why those images were circulated without consent (Lloyd, 2020). We need to challenge such regressive attitudes and beliefs that sustain abuse.

In the following section, we will explore various aspects of online infidelity, diverse ways in which people cheat online and possible reasons why they engage in such behaviors.

Internet infidelity: Secrets of happy and unhappy couples

Infidelity, online or offline, presents an ambiguous terrain. It is difficult to determine what comprises online infidelity. Does secretly watching pornography comprise online infidelity? Does browsing through Facebook images of a former partner comprise online infidelity? Or, does it start only when one starts communicating online with that person? Does chatting with an attractive colleague late in the evening comprise infidelity? What is the difference between chatting and flirting? When exactly can chatting be categorized as flirting?

Despite the ambiguity, several scholars have attempted to define both infidelity and online infidelity. Psychotherapist Brian Dianes defines infidelity as "interactions in a relationship in which at least one of the people engaging in it understands there to be a violation of agreed or implicit sexual and/or emotional boundaries within their couple relationship" (Daines, 2006, p. 48). To grasp infidelity issues, one therefore needs to understand not just the sociocultural context in which it is happening but also the moral and ethical compass of both the individuals apart from the "spoken and unspoken contract" couples have about loyalty and breach of trust (Daines, 2006).

Internet use introduces further complexities into the infidelity conundrum. Infidelity researchers, Hertlein and Piercy (2008) define Internet infidelity "as a romantic or sexual contact facilitated by Internet use that is seen by at least one partner as an unacceptable breach of their marital contract of faithfulness" (p. 484). To this definition, let us add the fact that Internet infidelity can happen not just within a marriage but in any committed relationship amongst people of any gender.

No matter how one defines Internet infidelity, one common element in various definitions is that of secrecy (Cravens & Whiting, 2014). For instance, people cheating online may quickly close the chat window when their spouse enters the room. They may delete their computer history or erase records of chats. They may even secretly message with a romantic partner when the spouse is in the same room. Basically, the online medium facilitates keeping an affair secret from the rest of the world (Cravens & Whiting, 2014).

Online and offline infidelity may be sexual, emotional, or a combination of both (Cravens & Whiting, 2014). Intimacy research shows that people tend to share their deepest thoughts while chatting with people online. Online chatting promotes uninhibited behavior and people may share more information than necessary. Users may end up discussing intimate details about their lives or spill personal secrets that even their primary partners have no idea about while chatting with someone online (Abbasi &

Alghamdi, 2017). Thus, online communication facilitates the development of emotional closeness amongst people.

However, emotional affairs can be as damaging as sexual affairs for married couples and those in committed relationships. In fact, emotional affairs are a common source of Internet infidelity (Abbasi & Alghamdi, 2017). For this reason, people often monitor their partners' social media usage. However, research indicates that partner surveillance may also lead to a relentless cycle of disappointment, insecurity, and increased monitoring (Abbasi & Alghamdi, 2017).

It has also been observed that couples tend to develop similar patterns of partner surveillance (Helsper & Whitty, 2010). If a person monitors his/her partner's online activities, there is a high possibility that the other person will also engage in similar behavior. On the other hand, if a person does not monitor his/her partner's online activities, it is very likely that the other person will also refrain from monitoring. Of course, several other factors are bound to influence surveillance patterns including the length of the committed relationship, socioeconomic background, and the age of the people in the relationship, amongst others (Helsper & Whitty, 2010).

Similarly, a multitude of factors would also influence the diverse ways in which people cheat on their partners online. In contemporary times, apps that facilitate extramarital affairs are highly popular. In the following pages, we will examine the use of such apps in a society such as India where open offline conversations about sex and sexual desires are rare.

Increasing use of extramarital apps: Just shake the device when your spouse looks your way

French extramarital affairs app Gleeden, which describes itself as a "discreet dating site made by women" claimed to have 8 lakh married Indian men and women registered for its services in January 2020 with most number of people registering from Bangalore (IANS, 2020). The reason for Bangalore being at the top of the list may be attributed to the city being home to a lot of tech-savvy people (Menon, 2020). Also, situations where working couples spend long hours at work and make frequent business trips create circumstances conducive to online infidelity.

Interestingly, the most active age group on Gleeden in India falls in the 34–49 years category and includes professionals such as doctors, lawyers, bankers, and senior executives (Dhawan, 2018). The app also has a "shake to exit" feature which one can use to disconnect immediately and close the app should the spouse or primary partner show up during a chat session.

In a survey conducted by Gleeden among 1,525 married individuals in India between the age of 25 and 50 living in several cities including Delhi,

Mumbai, Bangalore, Chennai, Hyderabad, Pune, Kolkata, and Ahmedabad, 49% married individuals admitted having an intimate relationship outside their marriage (Jha, 2020). In this sample, 53% married Indian women admitted to having an intimate relationship outside marriage compared to 43% men (Jha, 2020). Furthermore, 41% married Indian women admitted to regularly having sex with someone outside their marriage compared to 26% men (Jha, 2020).

If these figures are to be believed, more women in metros and other Indian cities are asserting their right to companionship and seem to be seeking affection outside their marriages than in previous years. Tellingly, a female Gleeden member told *The Week* news magazine that married Indian women join the extramarital dating service primarily for companionship as Indian men are usually non-communicative and rarely talk to their wives even as they remain busy "playing their socially-sanctioned roles" (Bhura, 2019).

When Ashley Madison, a Canadian "discreet" dating website, was hacked in July 2015, the leaked data also showed that the users in India were primarily women (Dhapola, 2015). Of course, the data could not be verified as many may be fake female profiles. However, the leaked data indicated that there were 2.7 lakh Ashley Madison users in India. The data was categorized according to geographical location and showed that the largest number of users in India were from Delhi followed by Mumbai (Dhapola, 2015).

While extramarital affairs have always been around, what appears to be changing is the degree of visibility they are garnering online. For instance, the Ashley Madison website carries a tagline, "Life is short. Have an affair." Meanwhile, the parent company of Ashley Madison also runs two other websites for related purposes. One of them, CougarLife.com, connects "modern, confident women with younger, energetic men" while the other, EstablishedMen.com, helps "young, beautiful women connect with older, generous men."

In case of India, it is paradoxical that despite the apparent rise in infidelity in India, the country has a 1% divorce rate. This indicates that Indian society expects spouses to forgive each other and continue under the same roof despite rampant extramarital affairs and cheating. In the Gleeden survey, 69% married individuals said that they expected their partners to forgive them for cheating (Jha, 2020).

Of course, the survey highlights opinions of tech-savvy people living in urban spaces and may not be indicative of mainstream discourses prevalent in the country. After all, one should not forget that India also witnesses honor killings in many towns and villages where young couples are murdered for falling in love and marrying outside the boundaries of caste, religion, and community. Such a restrictive social scenario probably contributes to more online communication between romantic partners. Let us now explore how the online medium facilitates intimacy-related interaction.

Inside an online chatroom: How can it be cheating if I don't touch my virtual partner?

Beatriz Mileham, a researcher at the University of Florida, studied how people cheat on their partners in online chat rooms and concluded that "never in history has it been so easy to enjoy both the stability of marriage and the thrills of the dating scene at the same time" (p. 11). The study involved in-depth interviews with 86 married participants and showed that not all participants behaved the same way in the chat rooms.

While some liked to keep it impersonal and focused on the act, others opened up about their lives and experiences creating an emotional connection with their virtual partner. This shows how online infidelity can take myriad forms and mean different things to different people (Mileham, 2007).

Most participants rationalized their chat room behavior and did not categorize it as infidelity as they did not physically touch their virtual partner. Many equated their activities in the chat room to reading a romantic novel or watching an adult movie discounting the fact that the latter are passive in nature while steamy chats require active participation.

Moreover, an important aspect of infidelity is betrayal. Psychotherapist Brian Daines explains the feelings involved in betrayal:

> The fundamental element in betrayal is that something is shared with another that is considered to belong exclusively to the public couple relationship. Important accompaniments are the sense that the partner has had something vital taken away from them and that the relationship has been diminished in a fundamental way. (p. 48)

If we accept this explanation, a person can betray his partner without being physically intimate with another person if his partner feels that something that should be exclusive to their relationship is no longer so.

In Mileham's study, those who accepted that their chatroom behavior amounted to cheating on their spouses attributed it to the lack of sex and affection in their marriages. The Internet helped them avoid their real-life problems and escape into a world of sexual fantasy.

Interestingly, amongst the chatroom participants were people who claimed to be "happily married" and very much in love with their spouses. These people rationalized their chatroom behavior as a consequence of their need for some excitement and fun (Mileham, 2007). More importantly, discussions in these chatrooms sometimes spilt over into people's real lives as evident by the fact that 30% of the participants eventually met their virtual partner offline and all except two engaged in sexual relations with them.

This study shows how difficult it is to keep boundaries between one's online and offline life as the two get intermittently interwoven. The outcome of online and offline infidelity is also similar. Like offline infidelity, online infidelity also leads to feelings of jealousy, betrayal, anger, loss, and mistrust (Cravens & Whiting, 2014).

People have not only expressed pain, shock, and anger about the intimacy their partners engaged in online with another individual but also about the lies they said to protect their double lives (Mileham, 2007). According to the American Association of Matrimonial Lawyers, many have cited increased and inappropriate use of Facebook by the spouse as a reason for divorce (Abbasi & Alghamdi, 2017). Online infidelity may also lead to domestic violence and poor sexual health (Fincham & May, 2017). This leads us to the million-dollar question: Why do people cheat?

No-risk relationships: Intimacy with robots and sex dolls

Media reports claim a rising trend of men getting intimate with sex dolls, especially in Japan and China (Allen, 2017). These life-sized dolls are made of silicone with ultra-realistic body parts. In 2017, around 2,000 such dolls were reportedly sold in Japan. Many Japanese men who buy these dolls claim they are unhappy in their relationships with real-life women while the dolls keep them happy as they never complain. Some Japanese men not only share their beds with their dolls but also take them out on dates (Allen, 2017).

In China, the gender gap has also contributed to men's fascination with sex dolls. It is predicted that China will have 30 million more men than women by 2030 due to the prevalent cultural preference for sons and restrictive population planning policies (Fong, 2017). Unlike the more expensive dolls produced in the United States that are capable of limited speech and body warmth, factories in China have been able to produce cheaper replicas with fewer features to suit every budget. While countrywide estimates of sex doll sales in China are not available, news reports claim that there has been a rise in sales in the country (Fong, 2017).

Meanwhile, a sex doll brothel has been opened in Spain that invites clients to try out their wildest sexual fantasies with them (Harper, 2017). These dolls are apparently disinfected with antibacterial soap after every use.

In the book *Alone Together: Why We Expect More from Technology and Less from Each Other*, MIT, professor Sherry Turkle (2011) refers to our contemporary fascination with robotic companions as the "robotic moment" where the "performance of connection seems connection enough" (p.9). The "technological promiscuity" we display seems to be an outcome of our refusal to deal with the complexities associated with real-life relationships.

Why do people cheat?

It's difficult to determine whether one turns to social media for intimate communication with someone other than one's real-life partner because the primary relationship has problems or if turning to social media causes problems in the relationship (Abbasi & Alghamdi, 2017). It seems both are possible. Comparing one's real-life partner with the carefully edited digital lives of others on Facebook, for instance, can lead to dissatisfaction with one's life and one's partner (Abbasi & Alghamdi, 2017).

While therapists often focus on communication problems amongst couples that might lead to online/offline infidelity, one also needs to examine the very nature of Internet technology and how it contributes to the issue. American researchers, Katherine Hertlein and Armeda Stevenson, outline the 7As that describe the characteristics of Internet technology that facilitate infidelity including anonymity, affordability, accessibility, approximation, acceptability, accommodation, and ambiguity.

We would all agree that the Internet helps users to project a preferred identity, one which highlights certain aspects of who we are and hides the rest. It can even facilitate the creation of a completely new identity with little connection to a person's real life. In terms of accessibility, one can access the Internet from just about anywhere without drawing too much attention. The Internet also offers experiences that are similar to real-life ones thereby blurring the line between fantasy and lived experience. It also offers a golden opportunity that one can use to go beyond one's lived experiences and realize one's wishes of what life could have been (Hertlein & Stevenson, 2010).

Basically, the Internet "accommodates" people's desires and expectations that cannot be realized in our everyday lives. Finally, Internet-related intimacy is inherently ambiguous as romantic partners may have radically different opinions about what comprises it. Apart from examining communication and trust issues that couples often face, it's important to understand how these 7As operate in people's lives to get better insight into their Internet-related intimacy problems.

Scholars who study infidelity have delineated individual and contextual factors that can facilitate it. Individual factors include personality traits such as neuroticism and narcissism; prior infidelity experience including exposure to infidelity in the parental family; a history of alcohol and/or drug abuse; psychological distress; and a permissive attitude toward casual sex (Fincham & May, 2017). Dissatisfaction with the primary relationship can also be a trigger. Contextual factors include a job that involves extensive travel which facilitates having an affair and keeping it secret from one's primary partner. While research shows more men cheat than women, the gender gap is closing (Fincham & May, 2017).

One may engage in online affairs to avoid the messiness of real-life intimacy and prefer the degree of control the Internet offers (Vossler, 2016). It is easy to imagine that the online partner has all the desirable qualities the primary partner supposedly lacks. Online infidelity may also cause tremendous confusion in the partner suffering it as they may wonder whether to end the relationship or not based on a virtual affair (Vossler, 2016).

Merely setting time limits on a partner's online activities at home may not help in the long run. Permanent solutions will require that the couple address problems in the relationship and resolve them (Vossler, 2016). Those who engage in online cheating may be in denial and they may require counseling and therapy to take responsibility for their actions.

While trying to understand varied approaches to infidelity, one must also keep in mind the fact that couples today have varied arrangements regarding intimacy. For instance, polyamory involves having two or more romantic relationships simultaneously. It is different from "swinging" where couples exchange partners for sexual intimacy. It is also not the same as an "open relationship" where two people who have a primary relationship with one another are free to get intimate with other people. Both in the case of swinging and open relationships, the additional relationships are considered secondary to the original one, unlike the situation in polyamory, at least, theoretically (Khokhar, 2019).

There seems to be a growing number of polyamorous people in India considering the increasing number of polyamorous Facebook groups that are spreading awareness about the practice including Polyamory India, Bangalore Polyamory, and Egalitarian Non-Monogamy, amongst others

(Khokhar, 2019). However, one must keep in mind that such complex intimacy arrangements require a high degree of transparency as they can easily lead to jealousy and resentment.

While some couples accept and promote intimacy outside marriage or the primary relationship, others follow a more traditional approach to intimacy and commitment (Daines, 2006). Then again, people may categorically denounce infidelity as morally wrong in public while their personal views on it may be more nuanced and complex (Daines, 2006). For instance, a person may justify his own acts of infidelity, while not giving the same kind of discretion to his partner. People may also compartmentalize their lives in unique ways to justify cheating on a partner.

Conclusion: The future of emotional intimacy and romantic commitment

In this chapter, we explored digital manifestations of love and lust and the need to view them in the context of contemporary practices rather than being narrow-minded and judgmental. With apps facilitating "hook ups," sexting, and extramarital affairs, there are bound to be concerns amongst some of us about the place of emotional intimacy in our lives today. One might wonder if we are losing our ability for emotional intimacy in real life because we want to be "safe" from heartache. But does heartbreak online cause any less pain?

It is possible that our dependence on apps and online networks for romantic intimacy highlights our desire for controlling every aspect of our lives as much as we can. We may be less equipped to deal with uncertainty today and prefer to delegate love and intimacy to our networked connections that can be switched off at any time we like.

Therefore, it is critical we find out where we would like to deploy our energies if we do not want to deal with the uncertainty and messiness of real-life relationships. Perhaps, the goal is to be more industrial and productive in our work lives. In fact, so many of us are so busy becoming "successful" that we are neglecting our basic need for human connection, affection, and understanding.

The world is at crossroads today. We still do not know whether the social isolation induced by the COVID-19 pandemic will change the way we live and relate to one another. Of course, news media have reported a growth in the use of dating and extramarital apps in India and elsewhere during the pandemic (Roy, 2020). The apps are also introducing new features during the lockdown to facilitate better online interaction.

But by the time the pandemic is over, will we reach for our apps more than we do today or will we connect with the person sitting next to us better?

More importantly, should we view this situation as being binary in nature? The answer to that question may be different for each one of us.

References

Abbasi, I. S. & Alghamdi, N. G. (2017). When flirting turns into infidelity: The Facebook dilemma. *The American Journal of Family Therapy, 45*(1), 1–14. doi: 10.1080/01926187.2016.1277804

Allen, F. (2017). My sex doll is so much better than my real wife. *New York Post.* Retrieved from https://nypost.com/2017/06/30/i-love-my-sex-doll-because-she-never-grumbles/

American Psychological Association. (2007). *Report of the APA task force on the sexualization of girls.* Retrieved from www.apa.org/pi/wpo/sexualization.html

Beware! Sexting can land you in trouble (2017, November 23). *The Times of India, Mumbai Mirror.* Retrieved from https://timesofindia.indiatimes.com/life-style/relationships/love-sex/Beware-Sexting-can-land-you-in-trouble/articleshow/49670245.cms

Bhura, S. (2019, March 30). Gleeden: An extramarital app by the women, for the women. *The Week.* Retrieved from https://www.theweek.in/theweek/leisure/2019/03/29/gleeden-an-extramarital-app-by-the-women-for-the-women.html

Bilton, N. (2014, October 29). Tinder, the fast-growing dating app, taps an age-old truth. *The New York Times.* Retrieved from https://www.nytimes.com/2014/10/30/fashion/tinder-the-fast-growing-dating-app-taps-an-age-old-truth.html

Brar, P., Dworkin, J., & Jang, J. (2018). Association of parenting with sexual attitudes and behaviors of college students in India. *Sexuality & Culture, 22*(4), 1037–1053. doi: 10.1007/s12119-018-9511-9

Chalfen, R. (2009). 'It's only a picture': Sexting, 'smutty' snapshots and felony charges. *Visual Studies, 24*(3), 258–268. doi: 10.1080/14725860903309203

Cooper, K., Quayle, E., Jonsson, L., & Svedin, C. G. (2016). Adolescents and self-taken sexual images: A review of the literature. *Computers in Human Behavior, 55*, 706–716. doi: 10.1016/j.chb.2015.10.003.

Cravens, J. D., & Whiting, J. B. (2014). Clinical implications of Internet infidelity: Where Facebook fits in. *The American Journal of Family Therapy, 42*(4), 325–339. doi: 10.1080/01926187.2013.874211

Daines, B. (2006). Violations of agreed and implicit sexual and emotional boundaries in couple relationships – Some thoughts arising from Levine's 'A clinical perspective on couple infidelity'. *Sexual and Relationship Therapy, 21*(1), 45–53.

Dhapola, S. (2015). Cheating website Ashley Madison hacked: Everything you need to know. *The Indian Express.* Retrieved from https://indianexpress.com/article/explained/what-ashley-madison-data-breach-means-who-it-impacts/

Dhawan, H. (2018, September 28). How infidelity thrives in the age of the Internet. *The Times of India.* Retrieved from https://timesofindia.indiatimes.com/home/sunday-times/how-infidelity-thrives-in-the-age-of-internet/articleshow/65997155.cms

Döring, N. (2014). Consensual sexting among adolescents: Risk prevention through abstinence education or safer sexting? *Cyberpsychology: Journal of Psychosocial Research on Cyberspace*, 8(1), Article 9. https://doi.org/10.5817/CP2014-1-9

Drouin, M., Ross, J., & Tobin, E. (2015). Sexting: A new, digital vehicle for intimate partner aggression? *Computers in Human Behavior, 50*, 197–204.

Fincham, F. D., & May, R. W. (2017). Infidelity in romantic relationships. *Current Opinion in Psychology, 13*, 70–74. doi: 10.1016/j.copsyc.2016.03.008

Fong, M. (2017, September 28). Sex dolls are replacing China's missing women. *Foreign Policy*. Retrieved from https://foreignpolicy.com/2017/09/28/sex-dolls -are-replacing-chinas-missing-women-demographics/

Halder, D., & Jaishankar, K. (2013). Revenge porn by teens in the United States and India: A socio-legal analysis. *International Annals of Criminology, 51*(1–2), 85–111.

Harper, P. (2017, October 27). Full of hot air. *The Sun*. Retrieved from https://ww w.thesun.co.uk/news/4779261/inside-the-barcelona-brothel-where-women-have -been-replaced-by-inflatable-dolls-so-randy-punters-can-fulfil-fantasies-they -wouldnt-dream-of-revealing-to-a-human/

Hasinoff, A. A. (2012). Sexting as media production: Rethinking social media and sexuality. *New Media & Society, 15*(4), 449–465. doi: 10.1177/1461444812459171

Helsper, E. J., & Whitty, M. T. (2010). Netiquette within married couples: Agreement about acceptable online behavior and surveillance between partners. *Computers in Human Behavior, 26*, 916–926.

Hertlein, K. M., & Piercy, F. P. (2008). Therapists' assessment and treatment of Internet infidelity cases. *Journal of Marital and Family Therapy, 34*, 481–497. doi: 10.1111/j.1752- 0606.2008.00090.x

Hertlein, K. M., & Stevenson, A. (2010). The seven "As" contributing to Internet related intimacy problems. *Cyber Psychology & Behavior, 7*, 207–230. Retrieved from http://cyberpsychology.eu/view.php?cisloclankuD2010050202&articleD1

Gupta, N. (2020, May 4). Bois Locker Room: Delhi schoolboys create group to share lewd photos, chats on classmates. *India Today*. Retrieved from https://ww w.indiatoday.in/india/story/bois-locker-room-delhi-schoolboys-create-group-to -share-lewd-photos-chats-on-classmates-1674303-2020-05-04

IANS. (2020, January 7). Nearly 8 lakh Indians are on extramarital app Gleeden and 'committed' to infidelity. *Businessinsider.in*. Retrieved from https://www .businessinsider.in/thelife/news/nearly-8-lakh-indians-are-on-extramarital-app- gleeden-and-committed-to-infidelity/articleshow/73662769.cms

Internet dating: 10 things I've learned from looking for love online (2015, November 15). *The Guardian*. Retrieved from https://www.theguardian.com/lifeandstyle /2015/nov/15/internet-dating-10-lessons-tinder

Jansen, M. (2020, April 14). The best dating apps for 2020. *Digitaltrends.com*. Retrieved from https://www.digitaltrends.com/mobile/best-dating-apps/

Jha, L. (2019). Online dating apps finding more love in India as user base triples in 2018. *Live Mint*. Retrieved from https://www.livemint.com/news/india/onli ne-dating-apps-finding-more-love-in-india-as-user-base-triples-in-2018-1560 186024202.html

Jha, L. (2020). 55% married Indians have cheated on their spouses, most are women: Survey. *Live Mint.* Retrieved from https://www.livemint.com/industry/media/55 -married-indians-have-cheated-on-their-spouses-most-are-women-survey-1158 2712240534.html

Kapur, M. (2020, April 14). Sexting can spice up your lonely lockdown days—only if you are careful. *Quartz India.* Retrieved from https://qz.com/india/1837215/t ips-for-safe-sexting-during-coronavirus-lockdown/

Kernsmith, P. D., Victor, B. G., & Smith-Darden, J. P. (2018). Online, offline, and over the line: Coercive sexting among adolescent dating partners. *Youth & Society, 50*(7), 891–904. doi: 10.1177/0044118X18764040

Khokhar, R. (2019, March 11). The truth about polyamory in India – 'It isn't about sex and fun.' *Scroll.in.* Retrieved from https://scroll.in/magazine/913801/the-tr uth-about-polyamory-in-india-it-isnt-about-sex-and-fun

Klettke, B., Mellor, D., Silva-Myles, L., Clancy, E., & Sharma, M. K. (2018). Sexting and mental health: A study of Indian and Australian young adults. *Cyberpsychology: Journal of Psychosocial Research on Cyberspace, 12*(2), article 2. doi: 10.5817/CP2018-2-2

Lloyd, J. (2020). Abuse through sexual image sharing in schools: Response and responsibility, *Gender and Education, 32*(6), 784–802. doi: 10.1080/09540253. 2018.1513456

Mallozzi, V. M. (2017, February 9). Girl meets boy, finally, after 9 years online. *The New York Times.* Retrieved from https://www.nytimes.com/2017/02/09/fashion/ weddings/vows-girl-meets-boy-finally-after-9-years-online.html

Matharu, A. (2020, May 4). Boys will be boys, if we stay silent about 'locker room' talk. *The Wire.* Retrieved from https://livewire.thewire.in/gender-and-sexuality/ boys-will-be-boys-if-we-stay-silent-about-locker-room-talk/

Menon, R. (2020, January 8). Bengaluru No. 1 in infidelity. *Deccan Herald.* Retrieved from https://www.deccanherald.com/metrolife/metrolife-your-bond -with-bengaluru/bengaluru-no-1-in-infidelity-792551.html

Mileham, B. L. A. (2007). Online infidelity in Internet chat rooms: An ethnographic exploration. *Computers in Human Behavior, 23*, 1–31.

Padte, R. K. (2015, April 2). Lounge opinion: Let's not call it porn. *Live Mint.* Retrieved from https://www.livemint.com/Leisure/ZLo2IxUsX5Ax4F4Wr G5LkO/Lounge-opinion-Lets-not-call-it-porn.html

Powell, A. (2010). Configuring consent: Emerging technologies, unauthorized sexual images and sexual assault. *Australian & New Zealand Journal of Criminology, 43*(1), 76–90.

Press Trust of India. (2004, December 28). DPS students suspended for sexually explicit MMS. *Hindustan Times.* Retrieved from https://www.hindustantimes .com/india/dps-students-suspended-for-sexually-explicit-mms/story-E3SdDp96 GgnPsyjRItNPaL.html

Ranzini, G., & Lutz, C. (2017). Love at first swipe? Explaining Tinder self- presentation and motives. *Mobile Media & Communication, 5*(1), 80–101. doi: 10.1177/2050157916664559

Roy, L. D. (2020, April 25). Covid no deterrent: Online dating soars amid lockdown; many pair up digitally. *Outlook.com.* Retrieved from https://www.outlookindia.

com/website/story/india-news-the-cupid-19-pandemic-online-im-yours-and
-youre-mine-theres-no-quarantine/351472

Sales, N. J. (2015, August 6). Tinder and the dawn of the "Dating Apocalypse".
Vanity Fair. Retrieved from https://www.vanityfair.com/culture/2015/08/tinder-
hook-up-culture-end-of-dating

Setty, E. (2019). Meanings of bodily and sexual expression in youth sexting culture:
young women's negotiation of gendered risks and harms. *Sex Roles*, *80*, 586–
606. doi: 10.1007/s11199-018-0957-x

Setty, E. (2020). 'Confident' and 'hot' or 'desperate' and 'cowardly'? Meanings of
young men's sexting practices in youth sexting culture. *Journal of Youth Studies*,
23(5), 561–577. doi: 10.1080/13676261.2019.1635681

Sumter, S., Vandenbosch, L., & Ligtenberg, L. (2017). Love me Tinder: Untangling
emerging adults' motivations for using the dating application Tinder. *Telematics
and Informatics*, *34*, 67–78.

Turkle, S. (2011). *Alone together: Why we expect more from technology and less
from each other*. New York: Basic Books.

Turkle, S. (2015). *Reclaiming conversation: The power of talk in a digital age*. New
York: Penguin Press.

Vossler, A. (2016). Internet infidelity 10 years on: A critical review of the literature.
The Family Journal: Counseling and Therapy for Couples and Families, *24*(4),
359–366.

Yashaswi, P. (2020, February 16). Indian women are swiping right for casual sex,
but are they getting it? *The Huffington Post*. Retrieved from https://www.huffingt
onpost.in/entry/indian-women-are-swiping-right-for-casual-sex-but-are-they-
getting-it_in_5e47c877c5b64ba2974ffa96

3 Self-tracking one's way to wellness

Expert patients, quantified health, and online communities

Lisa Adams tweeted and blogged about her cancer journey till death came at the age of 45 on March 6, 2015 (Larson, 2015). In one of her interviews, Adams mentions that she started writing out of emotional pain and the fear that she would die before her three children grew up. Her youngest child was 7 months old when she was first diagnosed with breast cancer at the age of 37. He was born with congenital defects and underwent corrective surgeries during the initial phase of her cancer treatment. Adams started blogging about how she simultaneously dealt with being both a full-time cancer patient and a stay-at-home mother (Haley, 2010).

Her decision to blog about her illness was influenced both by her father, a cardiothoracic surgeon, and by her mother, a psychologist. Additionally, her training in sociology and psychology helped her write about her experiences in a way that touched the hearts of many and informed them about the nature of the disease at the same time (Haley, 2010). She also wrote about relatable topics such as how to talk to children about having cancer and what should one say when a friend is diagnosed with cancer. Her blogs and tweets were highly popular.

Her Twitter profile @AdamsLisa is available even today. A review of her tweets would show that she had built a large interactive community of followers and friends. People responded to her tweets promptly and she engaged with them as well. Commenting on the high engagement visible on Adams' Twitter page in the *Duke Science Review*, Kristen Larson observed, "This is unique to social media, and it shows how community is created through instantaneous sharing of experiences, ideas and feelings irrespective of time and space."

While Adams considered her outpourings online to be both "therapeutic and altruistic," her writings and tweets became a source of public controversy when a high-profile journalist couple, Emma and Bill Keller, questioned the ethics of Adams' prolific and graphic sharing of her cancer journey on the Internet (Weber, 2015).

Labeling Adams as someone who was "dying out loud," Emma Keller (2014b), in an opinion column published in *The Guardian*, questioned if

Adams' tweets represented a case of "TMI" (Too Much Information) and if there should be boundaries in what one shares publicly. Her husband, Bill Keller (2014a), a former executive editor at *The New York Times*, compared his father-in-law's "honorable" and quiet death from cancer with Adams' "very public cage fight with death" in a subsequent opinion column.

What Bill Keller probably failed to account for was the wide difference in the age and circumstances of the two people he was comparing. Both Emma and Bill Keller's columns generated a huge backlash from Adams' social media followers and people at large even as some also came out in support of the Keller couple and their standpoints on the dignity involved in a quiet death from cancer. Of course, the author firmly believes that how one decides to cope with cancer or any terminal illness remains a deeply personal choice that nobody has the right to judge.

Whatever be the diverse positions on such a topic, Adams' chronicles on her cancer experience highlight how digital culture can make incredibly personal journeys highly public in nature. By the time Adams died, she had tweeted over 176,000 times and posted over 3,000 pictures online about her journey with cancer which included poetry apart from details about chemotherapy, mastectomy, and participation in drug trails (Larson, 2015).

In her accounts, she often offered graphic details of her treatment accompanied by names of medicines and the medical processes she had to undertake. For example, in February 2015, she wrote on Facebook: "Finishing up a 9-hour emergency trip in to urgent care center. Got platelets, magnesium, potassium, calcium, and THEN drained almost 3 liters of fluid from my abdomen" (Weber, 2015).

Adams is a good example of the proactive, "expert patient" who was "digitally engaged" and helped to create an online community of people living with cancer. In this chapter, we will start by exploring the concept of the "expert patient" and then examine contemporary digital health practices including seeking health information online and the widespread usage of self-tracking apps and wearable technologies by both patients and other individuals. We will then analyze how various types of health communities develop on the Internet and the functions they serve. Finally, we will discuss the response of doctors to such emerging digital healthcare practices and end with a discussion on the critical implications of such developments.

The expert patient: Proactive, responsible, and "digitally engaged"

The term "expert patient" was first used in England as part of a Department of Health initiative to manage patients with chronic illnesses (Shaw & Baker, 2004). This concept drew upon research in the United States on involving patients in managing chronic illnesses which reportedly led to better outcomes (Greenhalgh, 2009).

Proponents of the expert patient model believe it has the potential to empower patients by giving them a chance to contribute to decisions on their own treatment. They also hoped it would reduce medical paternalism and improve patient compliance (Badcott, 2005). Other commonly used terms for such proactive and well-informed patients include "autonomous patient," "involved patient," and "engaged patient" (Shaw & Baker, 2004).

With the increasing use of digital health technologies, the expert and participative patient began using digital devices to monitor his or her own health parameters such as blood pressure, cholesterol level, oxygen saturation levels, and so on, and report it to the medical practitioner. Critical health scholar, Deborah Lupton (2013), coined the term "digitally engaged patient" to refer to an expert patient who uses digital health technologies to monitor and care for his or her own health.

Contemporary healthcare policies encourage patients to use digital tools to monitor their health and practice self-care. Going beyond looking up health information on websites and participating in patient support groups online, patients are expected to use digital healthcare systems, wear digital devices that can monitor health parameters, use biosensors to facilitate managing of their medical conditions and disabilities, if any, consult with doctors using digital media, and share their experiences with others on digital platforms (Lupton, 2013). Thus, the role of the patient is changing from being "a minimally-informed advice recipient to an active participant, instigating collaborator, information sharer, peer leader and self-tracker engaged in participative medicine" (Swan, 2009, p. 513).

However, it is not just the role of the patient that is changing. Today, the nature of medicine is also changing from being an "art" with a focus on the haptic to that of both medical practitioners and patients collecting and using data on the human body (Lupton, 2013, p. 260). Digital healthcare assumes that more the data patients can collect on their bodies and share with their doctors, the more the control they can exercise on their illness.

Healthcare policies in many countries promote the ideal of the expert patient who engages in self-management of his/her own health using digital technologies (Greenhalgh, 2009). Many believe that health information systems have the potential to meet some of the healthcare challenges posed by growth in population, shortage of healthcare workers, rising costs of healthcare, increasing need for long-term management of chronic illnesses, etc. (Gibbons & Shaikh, 2016). India is one such country.

Although India's Internet penetration level is just over 40% (Diwanji, 2020), the government has launched many ambitious digital projects. In fact, health is an important aspect of the government's "Digital India" program that aims to transform the country into "a digitally empowered society and knowledge economy" (Government of India, n.d.). Even as the country suffers from large-scale poverty and inequalities in access to medical facilities, many amongst India's middle and upper classes demonstrate high levels of biomedical literacy and make every effort to gather health-related lifestyle information on the Internet and social media platforms (Broom et al., 2018).

With India's public health expenditure at merely 1.29% of its GDP in 2019–20 (Mehra, 2020), the current Indian government has repeatedly declared its intentions to use digital technologies to deal with longstanding healthcare challenges faced by the country, including a huge population, a stark rural-urban divide in terms of healthcare facilities, rise in chronic illnesses in the past few decades, shortage of doctors and nurses, and low insurance penetration, amongst others (Mishra, 2018).

Both physical and mental health issues amongst Indians are increasingly being framed as amenable to digital solutions (Mills & Hilberg, 2020). In 2016, the Indian government launched a "No-More Tension" app to help Indians manage stress (Taneja, 2016). People can use the app to measure their stress levels and use it to learn stress management techniques including yoga and meditation (National Health Portal, n.d.).

As part of its response to the COVID-19 pandemic, the Indian government launched the Aarogya Setu app in April 2020 with the declared purpose of tracing COVID-19 infections by using a smartphone's GPS system and Bluetooth. According to the government, the contract-tracing app reached 100 million subscribers in the first 40 days of being launched (Banerjea, 2020). Since the app collects substantial amount of personal and location information, it also raised privacy and security concerns amongst many people.

During the COVID-19 pandemic, the Medical Council of India (2020) formulated new guidelines on telemedicine practices in the country. The guidelines list the usage of video, audio, and text for telemedicine consultations and highlight the strengths and limitations of each mode. Like many other countries, the Indian government strives to promote multiple facets of digital healthcare in crisis and routine times.

In the following sections, we will discuss different aspects of contemporary digital health culture including activities undertaken by engaged patients and proactive individuals who closely monitor their lifestyles to meet specific health goals.

Seeking health information online: Googling before and after meeting doctors

Today, many of us turn to the Internet as our first source of health information. We search for our symptoms and attempt to self-diagnose before finally making an appointment with a doctor. After consulting with the doctor, some of us even search for the constituents and side-effects of the medicines prescribed for us.

Then there are those who relentlessly search the Internet for health information, engage in repeated self-diagnosis, and imagine that they are sick. More than 20 years ago, the news media coined the term "cyberchondriacs" for such people (Schmidt, 2019). Googling symptoms can make people more anxious, especially when a search for the word "headache" can bring up a potential diagnosis of brain tumor or a search for the phrase "perpetual fatigue" can suggest cancer as an underlying condition (Times News Network, 2018).

Of course, reading about a disease and feeling that one has all the associated symptoms predates the Internet. Here is an excerpt from the book *Three Men in a Boat* written by English author Jerome K. Jerome in 1889:

> It is a most extraordinary thing, but I never read a patent medicine advertisement without being impelled to the conclusion that I am suffering from the particular disease therein dealt with in its most virulent form.

When the protagonist approaches the doctor for a cure, he gets a prescription that includes nutritious food, regular exercise, and the following advice, "Don't stuff up your head with things you don't understand."

A study on health-information seeking on the Internet shows that those who are younger, more educated, have high socioeconomic status and the requisite Internet skills tend to look up health information on the Internet more than others (Jacobs et al., 2017). Apart from factors such as Internet accessibility, studies have also indicated that psychological factors such as anxiety about one's health and neuroticism might lead to greater online search for health information. Of course, the advantages of seeking health information on the Internet include easy accessibility, anonymity, and the potential for finding support online.

Older people with less education, low Internet skills, and socioeconomic status are more dependent on traditional media and healthcare professionals for health information than on the Internet. Thus, people who most need low-cost access to health information online are less likely to get it thereby indicating that sole reliance on digital technologies to disseminate health information may not yield desirable results and may even perpetuate inequalities in healthcare (Jacobs et al., 2017).

While seeking health information online can help a patient play a more active role in their treatment, trusting misleading, inaccurate, and irrelevant information can also be detrimental to their health and well-being. Since the trend of looking for health information online is here to stay, it's important to ensure that people have access to accurate information in "patient-friendly" formats (Tonsaker et el., 2014).

Physicians should also be open about guiding their patients to credible sources of health information. Healthcare providers should keep in mind that patients are inclined to trust sites that not only reflect medical expertise and lack of bias but also those that show awareness of their perspectives, issues, and concerns through FAQs and other methods (Sillence et al., 2007).

We will now discuss another common digital health practice prevalent all over the world which includes patients and other individuals using self-tracking apps and wearables to help them reach their health, fitness, and lifestyle goals.

Using self-tracking apps: Tracking health, sex, pregnancy, parenting, and more

Here is an example of a contemporary new year wish found on the Internet:

> May your hair, your teeth, your face-lift, your abs and your stocks not fall, and may your blood pressure, your triglycerides, your cholesterol, your white blood count and your mortgage interest never rise. (Wishquotes, n.d.)

While written in a humorous tone, it reveals the high level of health awareness prevalent amongst certain sections of society and the growing interest amongst them to monitor their own health closely. It also shows how common people have started adopting medical vocabulary. Increased health and lifestyle awareness have also led to the growing usage of health and fitness apps and wearable technologies.

Tracking health, fitness, and chronic illnesses

Health and Fitness apps and wearables can be used to track multiple health parameters. They are used not just for fitness purposes but for tracking chronic illnesses and mental health as well (Elflein, 2019). With more people using self-tracking apps and devices, various aspects of our lives such as physical activity, sleep patterns, and calorie intake are recorded on a regular basis. In March 2019, the top health and fitness app downloaded from Google Playstore was Calorie Counter by MyFitnessPal while the second most downloaded one was "Headspace: Meditation and Sleep" (Elflein, 2019).

Self-tracking may help to obtain highly relevant data about an individual's chronic condition including diabetes, hypertension, and obesity. Wearable devices offer specific benefits for those with chronic conditions as they can provide longitudinal data. For example, a wearable device can help determine the severity of symptoms of depression in a person by providing data on the number of conversations he or she has in a certain period, amount of physical activity and duration of sleep (Piwek et al., 2016). Similarly, body movement data can help diagnose early symptoms of Parkinson's disease in a person. Usage of pedometers can lead to an increase in physical activity among many.

According to Statista's report on "Fitness India", there were approximately 128 million fitness app users and 62 million wearable users in India in the year 2019. It is expected to grow significantly in 2020 due to the impact of COVID-19. The penetration rate for fitness apps and wearables in India is 9.3% and 4.5%, respectively, compared to the global penetration rate of 11.2% and 4.8%. More women (66%) than men use fitness apps and wearables in India and a significant portion of users (37%) belong to the 25–34 age group.

Tracking sex and reproductive activity

An analysis of self-tracking apps for sex and reproductive activities and functions shows how digital technologies influence the ways in which these aspects of life are experienced by people. Non-pornographic apps that track sexual activities offer myriad services such as tracking the duration and positions involved, the number of partners, the places where one had sex, the sound levels emitted during the act, etc. (Lupton, 2015). Apps for reproductive activities primarily track ovulation and menstrual cycles and may be used to facilitate conception.

While these apps can offer important insights into one's life, they also reinforce gender stereotypes, quantify male sexual performance, and convert physical intimacy into a "competitive and comparative" act (Lupton, 2015, p. 448). By quantifying sex, these apps view intimacy and reproduction in restrictive ways and may promote feelings of inadequacy in both men and women apart from reinforcing heteronormativity.

Also, users of such apps possibly do not realize the associated privacy risks. In 2011, Fitbit, a San Francisco–based company that sells activity trackers, wearables, and smartwatches, accidentally posted online data about its users' sexual activities that had been recorded as a part of their exercise routines (Lupton, 2015).

Tracking pregnancy and mothering activities

Pregnancy and mothering apps help women maintain dietary, fetal movement, and breastfeeding charts; follow an exercise regimen; and calculate pregnancy weight gain, amongst other things (Johnson, 2014). Of course, these apps are convenient as they provide easily digestible bits of information. But one wonders if such extensive tracking helps a pregnant woman or a new mother feel relaxed.

Mothers today are expected to not only have expert knowledge about their own health but also have quantitative and scientific data about their children, which may lead to cases of over-involved and intensive mothering (Johnson, 2014). Earlier, it was normal for mothers to offer subjective accounts about their children's health as they did not always have quantitative data to back up their feelings and intuition.

Unlike pregnancy apps for women that often adopt a serious tone, such apps for men tend to rely on humor to deliver their message. For example, a pregnancy app for men describes the size of the fetus by comparing it to the size of a football or a bottle of beer. Pregnancy apps for men also provide information on how to build a nursery and how to deal with finance and insurance after having a child. In many ways, these apps seem to be reinforcing gender stereotypes and inequalities in parenting (Johnson, 2014).

Quantified Self: Quantifying moods, illness, and health

In 2007, Gary Wolf and Kevin Kelly, both editors for *Wired*, an American magazine that showcases how technology affects our lives, started a website called the Quantified Self. It was the beginning of a movement that promoted self-awareness through tracking. The QS group describes itself as "an international community of users and makers of self-tracking tools who share an interest in 'self-knowledge through numbers.'" The members hold regular meetings and meet for two international conferences every year.

In Wolf's now-famous article published in *The New York Times* titled "The Data-Driven Life" (2010) which serves as a form of foundational text for the movement, he outlines the fundamental principle: "If you want to replace the vagaries of intuition with something more reliable, you first need to gather data. Once you know the facts, you can live by them."

For instance, one of the QS members tracked her grief after the sudden death of her mother by creating a "custom-made digital spreadsheet, where she could log various experiences related to her grief, including sights, conversations, and events that elicited memories of her mother" (Sharon, 2017, p. 110). She did not use any of the mood trackers available in the market and created her own "mood categories" instead. In this way, she felt free to experience grief in her own way without being influenced by social expectations and norms about how long one should mourn a loved one. It helped her cope with her own grief and help others going through similar phases in life.

Another famous QS member, Larry Smarr, discovered he had Chron's disease, which is a type of inflammatory bowel disease, after extensive self-tracking although his doctors had dismissed it. He was able to get the treatment he needed due to his own efforts (Sharon, 2017).

During the COVID-19 pandemic, the QS community launched a "Quantified Flu" project that would track the symptoms of the infection. The project members offered to analyze data obtained by wearable technology products for those who joined the project (Wolf, 2020).

Of course, the QS community cannot be taken as a representative of all those who use self-tracking devices. The members are highly qualified and are known to tweak their software to safeguard their privacy and interests even as several refuse to use proprietary software (Sharon, 2017).

Moreover, some scholars believe that since reports by QS members are single-subject reports, they cannot be used to determine the overall effectiveness of self-tracking devices that require longitudinal, randomized controlled studies (Piwek et al., 2016).

What we also need to realize is that the objective data obtained using these self-tracking devices and apps and the subjective, intuitive "feelings" that we all experience from time to time is not a zero-sum game (Sharon, 2017). Each type of knowledge has its own place and relevance. It is important to keep both the benefits and drawbacks of self-tracking devices and apps in mind and explore how people actually use them in their daily lives.

Privacy risks and other debates on apps and wearables

Extensive use of self-tracking devices and apps have led to debates around three primary issues (Sharon, 2017). While advocates of personalized healthcare view self-tracking devices such as fitness bands and related apps as "empowerment" tools for people, critics draw attention to the associated surveillance by corporations and the state. They highlight examples where companies have obtained data from self-tracking devices as part of wellness programs and linked it to determine insurance premiums for employees.

Secondly, advocates illuminate how usage of such devices promote overall health even as critics decry the disintegration of state and collective responsibility for maintaining health of populations. Thirdly, while advocates highlight that self-tracking devices and apps lead to greater self-awareness, others draw attention to its reductionist tendencies (Sharon, 2017). Self-tracking apps and wearable technologies reduce rich and complex phenomena into numbers and categories simultaneously displacing other "non-quantifiable yet highly insightful means of knowing and expression" (Sharon, 2017, p. 104).

It is important to note that while users own the wearable devices, they do not actually own the data they generate. Such data is owned by the company that makes the wearable device and may be sold to a third party. Simple anonymizing tactics may not help in obscuring the user's identity and location. The best way forward for the healthcare wearable sector would be to provide information to users about the nature of their data collection, storage, and usage (Piwek et al., 2016).

Moreover, it remains to be seen whether health and fitness apps and wearables are here to stay or represent a passing trend. Recent surveys indicate that 50% of users of wearable devices stop using them after a year. Some also report that usage of wearable devices requires too much effort and/or they do not like the user interface (Piwek et al., 2016).

Joining online health communities: Finding information and support

People with chronic conditions such as diabetes, arthritis, hypertension, and migraine join online health communities in search of support and information. People who live with stigmatized conditions such as mental illness, HIV, and cancer are more likely to look for both information and emotional support in online health communities (Maestre et al., 2018). The Internet not only provides a sense of anonymity, it also transcends limitations placed by time and place and helps to bring together people facing similar health issues.

Different online health communities meet different needs

A study on online health communities for people living with HIV indicated that while people sought more informational support in formal online forums that included healthcare providers, they looked for more emotional support in social, informal forums where they felt comfortable to openly express their feelings (Maestre et al., 2018).

Online health communities vary in nature, size, and purpose. For instance, a large Facebook group titled *Migraine.com* comprising more than 192,000 followers offers information, sympathy, and compassion to its members. A post encouraged those who suffer from migraine to take off their masks and not pretend that everything is fine at work and at home. Instead, people with migraine were encouraged to be upfront about their symptoms and seek help in managing the chronic neurological ailment (Lipson, 2019).

Online health communities such as *Migraine.com* offer emotional support in a myriad of ways including sharing of personal experiences, ways to manage the ailment, and even an occasional dose of humor. For instance, one of the questions posted on the group's Facebook page asked users if they had a nickname for their migraine which elicited some very funny and some not-so-funny answers.

In fact, ailment-related humor is used by several online groups to engage users and help them cope with their chronic conditions. *Endometriosis Memes* is one such Facebook group with approximately 15,000 members. Endometriosis is a gynecological ailment in which tissue that normally lines the uterus grows outside the uterus causing a lot of pain, bloating, and menstrual irregularities. This private online community describes itself as "a community for laughs about endometriosis" and clarifies that it is not a space for "support, advice, or questions."

In fact, the site administrators allow members to post only memes and jokes. Here is a sample of jokes and memes posted in the group: "Every morning I wake up in Spain. The S is silent." Another one carried a snippet of a conversation between a person with endometriosis and Fitbit, the fitness app: "Me: Exhausted. Fitbit: You have taken 9 steps today."

Different personas in online health communities

Looking at the nature of various online health communities, it is evident that people who join them have varying needs. Scholars have identified four different types of personas amongst users: Opportunists, scientists, adventurers, and caretakers (Huh et al., 2016).

Opportunists comprise users who are looking for very specific information. They skim forums and move on without engaging with the community members. Often, people who have been recently diagnosed with a health condition behave in this way. Those with "scientist" personas want to verify information posted on online health forums and would make very good site moderators. Adventurers often look for cutting-edge information about treatments and have a curious and open mind. Caretakers comprise those users who are emotionally invested in the community over a long period. They are usually experienced patients who offer advice to others about treatment regimens, etc. They also socialize with other members and offer emotional support (Huh et al., 2016).

However, most people read information posted on an online health forum and rarely contribute to it creating an information imbalance. Increasing bonds between members may encourage more people to share their views and experiences (Huh et al., 2016).

Since the narratives and information present in online health communities come directly from patients, they have become a new frontier in health research today (Bhowmick, 2016). They also keep patients informed about clinical trials and new drugs. Since people tend to trust others like them more than external authority figures, online health communities can greatly influence patient behavior and their compliance to treatment plans (Willis, 2014).

Online health communities develop on social media pages of doctors

Online health communities may also develop on the Facebook pages of doctors. For instance, the Facebook page of an infertility specialist in New Delhi has nearly 45,000 followers. Apart from the information posted by the doctor, members also share their experiences on it. The Facebook page also includes many pictures of patients posing with their babies at the end of a successful attempt. The members regularly interact with one another on these posts.

A study conducted by the author on why patients connect with physicians on Facebook in India revealed that three categories of people seek credible health information on doctors' Facebook profiles and pages: patients, caregivers, and healthy individuals (Mishra, 2019). Most of these people were highly educated and belonged to higher socioeconomic strata of society.

Many participants of the study felt that doctors do not give adequate information on preventive healthcare during face-to-face consultations and the Internet helped to locate such information. Unlike a Google search which may bring up unverified information, they believed that doctors' Facebook profiles or pages would have authentic information as their professional reputations were at stake (Mishra, 2019).

Being connected to a doctor on a social media platform such as Facebook also provided them psychological assurance, a sense of personal connect with the physician and access to an online community of people with similar experiences, especially in case of patients and caregivers.

To most of the participants of the study, health meant taking the right lifestyle decisions which would ensure they stayed fit, had nutritious food, and took adequate preventive healthcare measures. They also emphasized the need to control stress through meditation, regular exercise, counseling, and positive thinking. Many addressed increased anxiety about their health by opting for regular diagnostic tests (Mishra, 2019).

Some online communities operate outside and in opposition to medical science

Of course, not all online health communities operate within the traditional frameworks of medical knowledge. Some online forums may operate outside "medical guidance" or even in opposition to it. Digital technologies have myriad uses and can create multiple and diverse "health identities" amongst users (Fox & Ward, 2006).

For example, British researchers, Nick Fox and Katie Ward, observed that some online forums focused on the use of the drug Sildenafil (Viagra) and similar medicines provided information on how to buy the pills without a medical prescription so that the family doctor does not find out about the issue. Some users of the forum also encouraged non-medical uses of the drug for "hyper-normal" performance and even suggested it was good for use by women.

Similarly, some online forums including "pro-anorexia" groups operate through their "explicit opposition to a medical model of disease and treatment" (Fox & Ward, 2006, p. 471). While anorexia is considered unhealthy by medical practitioners, users of "pro-ana" groups considered it "aspirational" and discussed ways to make it sustainable. The members of the "pro-ana" group studied by the British researchers considered anorexia a safety net that would protect them from the emotional pain they felt in their everyday lives. Sustaining the anorexic body was the only way the members of the group believed they could control their environment.

It's important to note that the "health identities" discussed above are very different from that of the "expert patient." Instead of striving relentlessly to acquire medical knowledge and model their lifestyles around it, these identities reject such an ideal and operate outside conventional beliefs and expectations. However, such behavior is as much a part of digital health culture as the more commonly found models and practices.

For instance, anti-vaccination forums online are highly vocal about what they believe are adverse side-effects of vaccines. Since anti-vaccination activists are vociferous online, some pediatric clinics today even provide a guidebook to parents on "how to handle anti-vaccination attacks" (Leask

& Steffens, 2019). Meanwhile, a US-based study showed that parents may refuse to vaccinate their children due to four possible reasons: religious beliefs, personal beliefs, safety concerns, and the need for more information about a vaccine (McKee & Bohannon, 2016). Since pro-vaccination websites often use technical language, users may find it difficult to understand the information provided on them compared to the arguments made in online forums (Finnegan et al., 2018).

Now that we have explored various aspects of contemporary digital health culture in terms of patient-related activities and laypersons' practices, let us explore how doctors are coping with the emerging changes.

Medical degrees versus Google searches: Doctors' responses to emerging digital healthcare practices

These days, some doctors post the following message at their clinic's entrance or their office walls: "Don't confuse your Google search with my medical degree." This popular meme can also be found on mugs and other stationery items, often placed strategically in doctors' consultation chambers.

In response to this meme, this author found an interesting tweet that was "addressed to doctors everywhere" posted by jMac @Dex on January 26, 2019. It said: "Don't confuse the 1-hour lecture you had on my condition with my 20 years of living with it."

It is evident from such memes and tweets that the relationship between the patient and doctor is undergoing a churn. Many patients with chronic illnesses are resisting what they view as medical paternalism while doctors want patients to know that Google searches cannot replace their medical expertise.

An editorial in the *British Medical Journal* reveals that doctors often have a stereotypical view of the "expert patient" as someone who comes to consult with them carrying printouts from the Internet about their ailment and insists on a treatment that is unfamiliar to the doctor and unsuitable for the patient. They believe the "expert patient" would demand a lot of time from the doctor even as there would be a long queue of patients waiting outside (Shaw & Baker, 2004).

Doctors usually respond to Google-informed patients in one or two of the following three ways. They may feel insecure and highlight their own expertise as superior to any information found on the Internet. The doctors may also choose to collaborate with the patient and analyze the information the latter brings to the table. Furthermore, the doctor may even help the patient by providing information about credible health websites (McMullan, 2006).

Recent research shows that when people with serious illnesses find information related to their ailment on the Internet or other external sources and bring it to their doctors, they expect their doctors to give them a chance to discuss it (Garden & Seiler, 2017). When doctors with dominant communication styles prevented them from discussing such information, some patients even changed their doctors.

Despite all these changes, many doctors, especially in the West, are hesitant to connect with patients on social media. Katherine Chretien, a doctor at George Washington University, published an opinion column in *USA Today* requesting her patients not to send her "friend" requests on Facebook. She wrote:

> As your doctor, I might sit on the edge of your hospital bed and try to quell your fears and anxieties of being ill....We might sit together and catch up on your life over the past six months since we last saw each other. In fact, we might have a patient-physician relationship that makes other patients and physicians utterly jealous. But, please, don't ask me to be your friend. That is, your Facebook friend. (Chretien, 2010)

Concern about medico-legal issues, work overload, and the lack of reimbursement for online consultations are often considered to contribute to the rather hesitant adoption of online communication by medical practitioners (Katz & Moyer, 2004).

However, many patients have been vocal about wishing to connect with doctors over email and on social media platforms such a Facebook for some time now (Lee et al., 2015). Policymakers emphasize that physicians need to adapt to the changing role of the patient and shifts in the healthcare sector that demand greater sharing of healthcare information and medical decision-making. Physicians are increasingly expected to play the role of "a care consultant, co-creator and collaborator, generating health plans together with patients using the new tools" (Swan, 2009, p. 514–15).

In India, patients and doctors are increasingly connecting on WhatsApp and other social media platforms. Media reports mention doctors using social media apps including WhatsApp for counseling patients after surgery (IANS, 2015). This is particularly helpful for patients who live in areas located far from the hospital and return home soon after surgery. A hospital in Delhi has set up a WhatsApp group for patients living with cancer. Apart from patient care, hospitals and doctors are also using social media platforms to give lifestyle and health information (IANS, 2015).

In a recent study, the author interviewed doctors in India who are connected with patients on Facebook and found that they used the platform to communicate their personal brand and spread health awareness after adapting it to the Indian socio-cultural context (Mishra, 2018). Of course, the doctors remained anxious about possible trolling and medico-legal issues emerging from their online interaction with their patients.

To protect themselves, the doctors did not initiate contact with a patient on Facebook and did not offer specific medical advice on it either. They also ensured that they accepted Facebook "friend" requests only from patients whom they considered "intellectually mature" and "safe" to interact with. While doctors' concerns about connecting with patients on Facebook is completely understandable, such practices can reinforce existing inequalities in establishing access.

Several physicians also highlighted that they faced tremendous time constraints and did not have adequate knowledge about the usage of social media platforms. However, many doctors still believed that patients gained from connecting with them on Facebook and other social media platforms as it made them feel empowered and assured. They also pointed out that patients with chronic conditions stand to benefit the most from connecting with their doctor online (Mishra, 2018).

Doctors in other countries have also highlighted similar benefits to patients. For instance, Jordan Alpert and Frances Womble (2016), communication researchers at George Mason University, interviewed American physicians who use Twitter and found that although most of them did not send direct messages to patients, they believed that patients got a chance to be aware of their opinions and personalities on Twitter which facilitated some form of relationship-building between the two parties.

Critical implications: Interrogating narratives of "empowerment"

While acknowledging the benefits of digital health technologies, it is important to understand their implications on people and their lived experiences. What is projected as "patient empowerment" often translates into an additional set of duties that the patient must carry out including collecting data on their own illness at regular intervals and ensuring such data reaches the medical practitioners so that timely decisions can be taken. While some patients may find this empowering and liberating, others may find it overwhelming and tiring (Lupton, 2013).

The latter's resistance cannot always be attributed to technological incompetence as some patients may prefer personal rather than digital interaction with their healthcare providers. Moreover, some patients may be emotional about their illness and may not be able to regularly record data in a rational and disengaged manner. Instead, such patients may prefer that their doctors take control of their health so that they can lead less anxious lives (Lupton, 2013).

Kate Seear, an Australian researcher, interviewed women living with endometriosis, a painful and incurable gynecological condition, about self-management of their condition and its impact on their lives. Several women found the expert patient role they had adopted empowering and rewarding. However, others found the role of the expert patient overwhelming. They found endometriosis-related information on the Internet confusing and contradictory leading to more anxiety about their condition. They also found that the sheer amount of time spent in managing their own ailment drained them both physically and emotionally.

An excerpt from one of the respondent interviews in the study elucidates the point well:

> I think [the responsibility of managing your own health] is probably the hardest. I wish I could hand over my care to someone else and it would be like you sort out my health issues, you make me better in some way and I don't feel that there is anyone I can hand it to, but that I have got to do all of that. (Seear, 2009, p. 2010)

For women, who already complete a "first shift" at work, engage in a "second shift" doing household duties after returning from work, managing their own chronic condition and playing the role of the expert patient became their "third shift" (Seear, 2009, p. 202).

Similarly, Karen Sanders (2015) and her colleagues in Spain explored senior citizens' use and views of digital healthcare communication and found that while they valued the ability to look up health information online, they did not want to spend too much time online.

Thus, it is important not to blindly assume that usage of digital health technologies leads to empowerment of all patients. Instead, preferences of patients and their sociocultural values must be considered in determining appropriate usage. People manage chronic illnesses in the context of their social and professional roles and routines (Rogers, 2009). Apart from managing symptoms, people living with chronic ailments are also concerned with finding ways to live as much of a "normal life" as possible.

Also, illness management is rarely an individual work and involves one's family and interpersonal networks. Further, patients' expectations from treatment may vary based on the nature and stage of their illness (Rogers, 2009). All these factors need to be taken into account while envisaging the usage of digital health technologies and the idea of the expert patient.

Digital medicine also carries important implications for medical practitioners as they may have to treat patients who provide a lot of "data" virtually but little contextual clues about their specific situation (Lupton, 2013). Additionally, doctors need to be prepared for more people bringing wearable device data to their clinical consultations (Piwek et al., 2016).

Since digital healthcare practices privilege measurement and quantification, patients are also encouraged to rate their doctors. While rating doctors may offer certain benefits such as increasing accountability and empowering patients, it also has major drawbacks. Doctors may "overprescribe and overtest" to "satisfy" a patient and obtain high scores (Falkenberg, 2013). Studies have also indicated that patient satisfaction may not be a reliable indicator of good medical care. Also, while patients may be good at evaluating overall medical facilities, we need to explore whether patients are qualified to judge specific types of medical care (Falkenberg, 2013).

Moreover, while it may be easy to agree on the criteria that can help categorize a restaurant or a salon as "good," it is difficult to agree on what makes a "good" doctor. For example, while waiting time may be considered an important criterion while choosing a general practitioner, it is irrelevant while choosing a specialist such as a cardiac surgeon (Petrow, 2017). In case of a cardiac surgeon, one may need to explore their success rate and professional experience as well. Then again, including these parameters to rate a cardiac surgeon may still be inadequate. Therefore, using online ratings to choose a doctor, if used at all, should be combined with recommendations from friends, relatives, or other doctors.

Overall, it is important for people to realize that the Internet can be a source of highly unreliable information on healthcare and associated practices including the usage of medicines and their side effects. The COVID-19 pandemic has added fuel to the ongoing corporate battles about the efficacy of specific medicines that are fought in both offline and online spaces and are characterized by intense lobbying and trolling. Historically, Big Pharma groups have accused Indian companies of violating patent law and selling low-quality drugs even as India remains a leading supplier of generic medicines worldwide (Koppikar-Moorthy, 2020).

Conclusion

Before we conclude this chapter, we must ask ourselves what "health" means to us today. Does it comprise walking 10,000 steps a day? Does it mean ensuring that we are in the "normal" range on all the parameters that our digital devices record? Is health about getting all-body diagnostic check-ups twice a year? Did our parents and grandparents view "health" differently than we do? As digital technologies become an integral aspect of contemporary healthcare, we need to explore the changing meanings of health that privilege self-monitoring, self-care, and preventive medicine and its related implications.

There is nothing wrong with privileging lifestyle factors as a critical determinant in maintaining our health. But the problem starts when we view "health" in purely individualistic terms and consider it a consequence of lifestyle decisions alone. When we adopt such a limited approach, we ignore the socioeconomic and structural factors that contribute to illness (Dutta & Zoller, 2008). For example, when we view stress as something that can be managed with individual lifestyle choices alone such as yoga, meditation, and psychological counseling, we ignore the "structural inequalities and socio-economic circumstances underlying the growing incidence of tension" (Gooptu & Krishnan, 2017, p. 404).

Moreover, ignoring systemic and structural factors will not improve the state of healthcare of large sections of people. The COVID-19 pandemic has certainly highlighted the need for society and the state to take collective responsibility for citizens' health and well-being. It has also highlighted the need for the state to invest in public health infrastructure.

While it is evident that digital healthcare can play a significant role in reducing India's increasing chronic disease burden, we must not forget that not all health issues have digital solutions. We cannot recommend technology-based solutions without analyzing the lived experiences and practices of people.

We also cannot ignore digital divides. Not everybody can afford digital devices or have the luxury to engage in continual self-monitoring. Individual experiences of illness in India can be vastly different for different people based on their socioeconomic background, cultural and religious beliefs, and availability of medical care facilities in their area, amongst other factors (Broom et al., 2018).

Therefore, we need to be open to the creative uses of technology while simultaneously paying attention to actual experiences of people, how they view illnesses and the value they place on interpersonal networks of caregiving that may not be compatible with large-scale digitization (Mills & Hilberg, 2020). As India takes leaps in digital healthcare, it also needs to introduce adequate data privacy regulations that cater to the country's specific needs. Finally, while considering the emancipatory possibilities of digital health technologies, we cannot ignore its surveillance capabilities and discriminatory tendencies.

References

Alpert, J. M., & Womble, F. E. (2016). Just what the doctor tweeted: physicians' challenges and rewards for using twitter. *Health Communication, 31*(7), 824–32.

Badcott, D. (2005). The expert patient: Valid recognition or false hope? *Medicine, Health Care Philosophy, 8*, 173–178. doi: 10.1007/s11019-005-2275-7

Banerjea, A. (2020, May 26). Aarogya Setu identified over 3,000 Covid-19 hotspots in 3–17 days ahead of time: Kant. *Livemint.com*. Retrieved from https://www.liv emint.com/technology/tech-news/coronavirus-update-aarogya-setu-identified -over-3-000-covid-19-hotspots-in-3-17-days-ahead-of-time-kant-1159050306 0663.html

Bhowmick, A. A. (2016, August 26). Online health communities: A new frontier in health research. *Medium.com*. Retrieved from https://medium.com/@ abhowmick1/online-health-communities-a-new-frontier-in-health-research -71fb73edbea2

Broom, A., Kenny, K., Bowden, V., Muppavaram, N., & Chittem, M. (2018). Cultural ontologies of cancer in India. *Critical Public Health, 28*(1), 48–58. doi: 10.1080/09581596.2017.1288288

Chretien, K. C. (2010). A doctor's request: please don't 'friend' me. *USA Today*. Retrieved from https://usatoday30.usatoday.com/news/opinion/forum/2010-06 -10-column10_ST1_N.htm#

Diwanji, S. (2020). Number of internet users in India 2015–2023. *Statista.com*. Retrieved from https://www.statista.com/statistics/255146/number-of-internet-u sers-in-india/

Dutta, M. J., & Zoller, H. M. (2008). Theoretical foundations: Interpretive, critical and cultural approaches to health communication. In H. M. Zoller & M. J. Dutta (Eds.), *Emerging perspectives in health communication: Meaning, culture and power* (pp. 1–27). New York: Taylor & Francis.

Elflein, J. (2019, August 9). Share of people worldwide who used technology to track their fitness 2016, by age. *Statista.com*. Retrieved from https://www.statista .com/statistics/742448/global-fitness-tracking-and-technology-by-age/

Falkenberg, K. (2013). Why rating your doctor is bad for your health. *Forbes.com*. Retrieved from https://www.forbes.com/sites/kaifalkenberg/2013/01/02/why-ra tingyour-doctor-is-bad-for-your-health/#6db8d15633c5

Finnegan, G., Holt, D., & English, P. M. (2018). Lessons from an online vaccine communication project. *Vaccine, 36*(44), 6509–6511. doi: 10.1016/j. vaccine.2018.05.007

Fitness India. *Statista.com*. Retrieved from https://www.statista.com/outlook/313 /119/fitness/india

Fitness worldwide. *Statista.com*. Retrieved from https://www.statista.com/outlook /313/100/fitness/worldwide#market-users

Fox, N., & Ward, K. (2006). Health identities: From expert patient to resisting consumer. *Health: An Interdisciplinary Journal for the Social Study of Health, Illness and Medicine, 10*(4), 461–479. doi: 10.1177/1363459306067314

Garden, R. L., & Seiler, W. J. (2017). Serious illness conversations with doctors: Patients using information obtained from sources other than their doctors. *Health Communication, 32*(1), 22–31. doi: 10.1080/10410236.2015.1092061

Gibbons, M. C., & Shaikh, Y. (2016). The patient of the future: Participatory medicine and enabling technologies. In Weaver, CA, Ball, M. J., Kim, G. R., & Keil, J. M. (Eds), *Healthcare information management systems: Cases, strategies, and solutions* (pp. 283–297). 4th ed. Springer, Baltimore, Maryland.

Gooptu, N., & Krishnan, S. (2017). Tension. *South Asia: Journal of South Asian Studies, 40*(2), 404–406.

Government of India. (n.d.). *About Digital India.* Retrieved from https://digitalindia .gov.in/

Greenhalgh, T. (2009, March 14). Chronic illness: Beyond the expert patient. *British Medical Journal, 338,* 629–631.

Haley (2010, August 16). *Lisa Bronchek Adams, Stay at home mother & blogger: Words from a survivor.* Retrieved from http://nocountryforyoungwomen.com/2 010/08/16/lisa-stay-at-home-mother-blogger-words-from-a-survivor/

Huh, J., Kwon, B. C., Kim, S., Lee, S., Choo, J., Kim, J., Choi, M., & Yie, J. S. (2016). Personas in online health communities. *Journal of Biomedical Informatics, 63,* 212–225.

Indo-Asian News Service. (2015). Whatsapp, doc? Social media becomes a new platform for social media advice. *Firstpost.com.* Retrieved from https://www .firstpost.com/living/whatsapp-doc-social-media-becomes-a-new-platform-for -medical-advice-2333024.html

Jacobs, W., Amuta, A. O., & Jeon, K. C. (2017). Health information seeking in the digital age: An analysis of health information seeking behavior among US adults. *Cogent Social Sciences, 3*(1), 1302785. https://www.tandfonline.com/ doi/pdf/10.1080/23311886.2017.1302785?needAccess=true. doi: 10.1080/2331 1886.2017.1302785

Johnson, S. A. (2014). "Maternal devices," social media and the self-management of pregnancy, mothering and child health. *Societies, 4,* 330–350. doi: 10.3390/ soc4020330

Katz, S. J., & Moyer, C. A. (2004). The emerging role of online communication between patients and their providers. *Journal of General Internal Medicine, 19*(9), 978–83.

Keller, B. (2014a, January 12). Heroic measures. *The New York Times.* Retrieved from   https://www.nytimes.com/2014/01/13/opinion/keller-heroic-measures .html

Keller, E. G. (2014b, January 8). Forget funeral selfies. What are the ethics of tweeting a terminal illness? *The Guardian.* Retrieved from https://www.theguar dian.com/commentisfree/2014/jan/08/lisa-adams-tweeting-cancer-ethics

Koppikar-Moorthy, A. (2020). Understanding the coming challenges to India's pharma sector. Retrieved from https://www.orfonline.org/expert-speak/unders tanding-the-coming-challenges-to-indias-pharma-sector-66556/

Larson, K. (2015). Autopathography and online community: Applying biovalue to understand the Lisa Adams controversy. *Duke Science Review.* Retrieved from http://dukesciencereview.com/issues/3

Leask, J., & Steffens, M. (2019). Four ways to talk with vaccine skeptics. *The Conversation.* Retrieved from https://theconversation.com/4-ways-to-talk-with -vaccine-skeptics-125142

Lee, J., Choudhry, N. K., Wu, A. W., Matlin, O. S., Brennan, T. A., & Shrank, W. H. (2015). Patient use of email, Facebook, and physician websites to communicate with physicians: A national online survey of retail pharmacy users. *Journal of General Internal Medicine, 31*(1), 45–51.

Lipson, S. (2019). Taking off the mask: The real face of migraine. *Migraine.com*. Retrieved from https://migraine.com/living-migraine/taking-off-mask/

Lupton, D. (2013). The digitally engaged patient: Self-monitoring and self-care in the digital health era. *Social Theory & Health, 11*(3), 256–270.

Lupton, D. (2015). Quantified sex: A critical analysis of sexual and reproductive self-tracking using apps. *Culture, Health & Sexuality: An International Journal for Research, Intervention and Care, 17*(4), 440–453. doi: 10.1080/13691058.2014.920528

Maestre, J. F., Herring, S. C., Min, A., Connelly, C. L., & Shih, P. C. (2018). Where and how to look for help matters: Analysis of support exchange in online health communities for people living with HIV. *Information, 9*, 259–274.

McKee, C., & Bohannon, K. (2016). Exploring the reasons behind parental refusal of vaccines. *The Journal of Pediatric Pharmacology and Therapeutics, 21*(2), 104–109.

McMullan, M. (2006). Patients using the Internet to obtain health information: How this affects the patient–health professional relationship. *Patient Education and Counseling, 63*, 24–28.

Medical Council of India. (2020). Telemedicine practice guidelines. Retrieved from https://www.mohfw.gov.in/pdf/Telemedicine.pdf

Mehra, P. (2020, April 8). India's economy needs big dose of health spending. *Livemint.com*. Retrieved from https://www.livemint.com/news/india/india-s-economy-needs-big-dose-of-health-spending-11586365603651.html

Mills, C., & Hilberg, E. (2020). The construction of mental health as a technological problem in India. *Critical Public Health, 30*(1), 41–52. doi: 10.1080/09581596.2018.1508823

Mishra, S. (2018). When patients connect with physicians on Facebook: Physician perspectives on benefits, challenges, and strategies for managing interaction. *Health & Technology, 9*(4), 505–515.

Mishra, S. (2019). *Looking for medical advice in everyday digital spaces: A qualitative study of indians connecting with physicians on Facebook.* Presented at the 2nd International Conference on Digital Economy (ICDE). IIM Raipur, December 6–8, 2019.

National Health Portal. (n.d.). No more tension. Retrieved from https://www.nhp.gov.in/mobile-no-more-tension

Petrow, S. (2017, December 2). Why online reviews are not the best way to choose a doctor? *The Washington Post*. Retrieved from https://www.washingtonpost.com/national/health-science/why-online-reviews-are not-the-best-way-to-choose-a-doctor/2017/12/01/f2be27b8-c4a7-11e7-afe9 4f60b5a6c4a0_story.html

Piwek, L., Ellis, D. A., Andrews, S., & Joinson, A. (2016). The rise of consumer health wearables: Promises and barriers. *PLoS Medicine 13*(2), e1001953. doi: 10.1371/journal.pmed.1001953

Rogers, A. (2009). Advancing the expert patient. *Primary Health Care Research & Development, 10*, 167–176. doi: 10.1017/S1463423609001194

Sanders, K., Valle, M. S., Vinaras, M., & Llorente, C. (2015). Do we trust and are we empowered by "Dr. Google"? Older Spaniards' uses and views of digital healthcare communication. *Public Relations Review, 41*, 794–800.

Schmidt, C. (2019, April 5). Cyberchondriacs just know they must be sick. *Scientific American*. Retrieved from https://www.scientificamerican.com/article/cyberch ondriacs-just-know-they-must-be-sick/

Seear, K. (2009). The third shift: Health, work and expertise among women with endometriosis. *Health Sociology Review, 18*(2), 194–206. doi: 10.5172/ hesr.18.2.194

Sharon, T. (2017). Self-tracking for health and the quantified self: Re-articulating autonomy, solidarity, and authenticity in an age of personalized healthcare. *Philosophy & Technology, 30*, 93–121. doi: 10.1007/s13347-016-0215-5

Shaw, J., & Baker, M. (2004). "Expert patient" – Dream or nightmare. *British Medical Journal, 328*(7442), 723–724. doi: 10.1136/bmj.328.7442.723

Sillence, E., Briggs, P., Harris, P. R., & Fishwick, L. (2007). How do patients evaluate and make use of online health information? *Social Science & Medicine, 64*, 1853–1862.

Swan, M. (2009). Emerging patient-driven health care models: An examination of health social networks, consumer personalized medicine and quantified self-tracking. *International Journal of Environmental Research and Public Health, 6*, 492–525. doi: 10.3390/ijerph6020492

Taneja, R. (2016, November 14). Stressed? Government has a mobile app for that. *NDTV.com*. Retrieved from https://everylifecounts.ndtv.com

Times News Network. (2018). Your habit of Googling your symptoms is bad for your health. *The Times of India*. Retrieved from https://timesofindia.indiatime s.com/life-style/health-fitness/health-news/your-habit-of-googling-your-sym ptoms-is-bad-for-your-health/articleshow/66333213.cms

Tonsaker, T., Bartlett, G., & Trpkovm, C. (2014). Health information on the Internet Gold mine or minefield? *Canadian Family Physician, 60*, 407–408.

Weber, B. (2015, March 9). Lisa Bonchek Adams dies at 45; Chronicled fight with breast cancer. *The New York Times*. Retrieved from https://www.nytimes. com/2015/03/10/health/lisa-bonchek-adams-dies-at-45-chronicled-fight-with-breast-cancer.html

Willis, E. (2014). The making of expert patients: The role of online health communities in arthritis self-management. *Journal of Health Psychology, 19*(12), 1613–1625. doi:10.1177/1359105313496446

Wishquotes. (n.d.). Retrieved from https://www.wishesquotes.com/new-year/happy -new-year-wishes

Wolf, G. (2010). The data-driven life. *The New York Times*. Retrieved from https:// www.nytimes.com/2010/05/02/magazine/02self-measurement-t.html

Wolf, G. (2020, May 27). *Self-tracking for Covid-19*. Retrieved from https://quantif iedself.com/blog/self-tracking-for-covid-19/

4 Becoming Internet famous

Performing "authenticity" and engaging audiences

What do you want to be when you grow up? When Toy production company Lego asked this question to 3,000 children between the ages of 8 and 12 from the United States and the United Kingdom, their answers surprised them. The top career choice for children in the United States and United Kingdom was a vlogger or YouTuber followed by teacher, professional athlete, musician, and astronaut (Taylor, 2019). Becoming famous on the Internet for the videos one makes is a coveted dream amongst many young people today.

The Internet has facilitated the emergence of celebrities on different platforms including YouTube, Instagram, Twitter, and Facebook, amongst others. These celebrities are known as "YouTube stars," "Instafamous," or just "Internet famous" in popular parlance and "microcelebrities" in academic literature.

Theresa Senft, a researcher in performance studies, coined the term "micro-celebrity" in 2001 when she was researching how "camgirls" used online tools for what was then considered a new style of performance to connect with their audience (Khamis et al., 2017). Camgirls or Webcam models, who performed live on the Internet, adopted self-branding strategies that are very similar to what Internet celebrities adopt today.

In 1996, Jennifer Ringley was the first women to showcase her life online by allowing people to view her daily life including sexual acts by installing a Webcam in her college dorm room in the United States. The website "JenniCam" became highly popular and she continued streaming for 7 years before she disappeared from the spotlight completely (Baldwin, 2004).

On most days, her appeal was her ordinariness. For example, people could log in on Saturday nights while doing laundry and see Jenny doing the same as well. To her viewers, she represented "real life." A strong community also grew in her chatroom on her website as she was accessible online – a concept that was new to people at that time (Krotoski, 2016). People did not really know her but could connect with her all the same.

Webcam streaming by "camgirls" represents an early version of the genre that became reality television because of its perceived focus on the "real" (Khamis et al., 2017). Ordinary people became stars by participating in shows such as Big Brother, American Idol, and Master Chef. The life struggles of the participants were presented as relatable to the experiences of the viewers.

While the background, story, and pitch of successful participants on reality shows had to match the brand's narrative and values of the target audience, social media removed all such constraints as anyone could blog, vlog, tweet, or post online and find their niche audience. Social media made it possible for ordinary people to potentially reach a large audience without the blessings of an editor or producer. To start, all they needed was a good idea. The arduous task of getting people's attention and sustaining it would come at a later stage.

In her book *Camgirls: Celebrity and Community in the Age of Social Networks*, Theresa Senft defines microcelebrity as "a new style of online performance in which people employ webcams, video, audio, blogs, and social networking sites to 'amp up' their popularity among readers, viewers, and those to whom they are linked online" (p. 25).

This chapter explores several case studies of microcelebrities both in India and abroad. An attempt has been made to include microcelebrities from various genres of vlogging such as beauty and lifestyle, gaming, comedy, and cooking. Before engaging with the case studies, we will examine some of the differences between traditional celebrities and Internet celebrities although the features integral to both the categories are in a constant state of flux.

Traditional celebrities versus microcelebrities: Choreographing "ordinariness"

Unlike traditional celebrities, who are rarely accessible and have to be chased by the paparazzi for a picture that would find favor with the fans, those who are Internet famous often present themselves as available and accessible online. Internet celebrities constantly create and upload content on online platforms and their audiences respond with likes, comments, and shares. Of course, traditional celebrities also upload their videos on various social media platforms. But micro-celebrities engage in a specific type of performance online.

They work hard to portray an authentic image so their followers can relate to them and their online content. Performance of authenticity refers to a "highly choreographed style of authentic and amateur self-presentation that ultimately bears no relation to the skill level or professionalism of the influencer employing it" (Bishop, 2019, p. 28).

Authenticity often involves revealing intimate details about one's private life. Many influencers believe they have to Instagram, tweet, Facebook, blog, or YouTube every event in their life. In fact, microcelebrity culture is based on the belief that an event has not happened unless it has been digitally documented and posted online. Only after the photos are taken and posted online do influencers start relaxing and enjoying an event (Mavroudis, 2019). Of course, such practices are hardly restricted to Internet celebrities. Many ordinary people behave in a similar fashion today.

However, authenticity may not always mean revealing personal details about one's life. It may also mean being consistent about the image one presents online (Marwick, 2013). Digital influencers and microcelebrities ensure that they do not post anything that contradicts the image they have created online (Mavroudis, 2019).

Microcelebrity scholar Jonathan Mavroudis calls the work that Internet celebrities engage in as "fame labour" which refers to the "invisible, emotional work" that goes into maintaining their online persona and status (p. 86). Being a microcelebrity is labor intensive. It involves coming up with content ideas, creating content, and maintaining online popularity by satisfying one's audience. Microcelebrities do not automatically become digital influencers unless they obtain "brand endorsement status" apart from having a large number of followers and a strong collaborative network of other digital influencers (Mavroudis, 2019, p. 86).

People practice microcelebrity in multiple ways. While some actively interact with their audiences by responding to their comments, etc., others may not. Although the videos depict Internet celebrities talking to viewers in a style that is similar to the way we talk with close friends, the "close relationship" that develops between Internet celebrities and their viewers is para-social in nature, that is, it is both imaginary and one-sided (Fägersten, 2017).

When microcelebrities garner enough fans, manage to get lucrative business deals and expand their business by launching products, etc., they may migrate into the sphere of traditional celebrities. Such transformations often create a tension between their performance of authenticity and ordinariness and the practices of traditional celebrityhood, which involve keeping fans at a distance and being inaccessible (Jerslev, 2016).

While YouTube presents one of the most visible platforms where Internet celebrities are born, people have attained celebrityhood on other platforms as well. Different platforms inspire different microcelebrity practices. For instance, microcelebrities on Twitter may prioritize a style of presentation that is different from what is preferred on Instagram, which is a highly visual medium. In case of Instagram, ordinary users have attained "Instafame" by posting eye-catching selfies and other digital images. Those who are

"Instafamous" are basically "famous for being famous," that is, they are famous for their ability to attract attention of other users (Marwick, 2015, p. 149).

In the following section, we will analyze the case of well-known UK-based YouTuber, Zoe Elizabeth Sugg, who is known as "Zoella" on YouTube and the techniques she uses to connect with her target audience.

Zoella: Connecting with millions with beauty and lifestyle videos

Zoe Elizabeth Sugg has been uploading videos on YouTube since 2009. She started with her beauty and lifestyle channel called "Zoella" and launched another channel that focused on day-in-the-life videos called "More Zoella" in 2012 (Jerslev, 2016). Zoella is considered UK's wealthiest female social media star under 30. In 2019, she made £ 600,000 a year from her two life-style channels and gets paid £ 12,000 for a single sponsored Instagram post (Griffin, 2019).

Zoella's father is a property developer and her mother is a beautician. One of the reasons she decided not to attend university was because of anxiety issues, a topic she has discussed in her vlogs. She started her journey on social media with a blog on beauty and fashion. After creating a successful audience for her blog, she moved over to vlogging. Initially, she focused on the 13–20 age group but she now vlogs for the "millennial woman" (Ford, 2014).

Zoella performs authenticity by declaring that she is sharing her real and private life with everyone else. She addresses her fans directly as "you guys" and presents herself as an "honest and unpretentious" person (Jerslev, 2016). She also uses a confessional style in some of her videos. Examples include her videos on anxiety and panic attacks and how she feels over-whelmed at times.

She may ask for the advice from her fans on a particular piece of cloth-ing she purchased. A traditional celebrity, let's say, Bollywood star, Katrina Kaif, would not really ask for her fans' advice on what to wear. Zoella often declares her love for her fans in her videos as if they were not millions of people whose names she does not know but a small circle of close friends (Jerslev, 2016).

Her videos include "errors" that she might have made during filming (Jerslev, 2016). These chance happenings might include a dog walking in and barking in the middle of her filming or her boyfriend making an inad-vertent remark from elsewhere in the house. Also, the lighting in the video may change when the sun goes behind cloud or comes out of one. All these features lend a sense of authenticity and spontaneity to her vlogs.

In 2014, Zoe Sugg published her first novel "Girl Online" which ran into controversy when she was accused of ghostwriting it. She responded with a video where she mentioned taking help from others as it was her very first time writing a book (Jerslev, 2016). In 2015, she released her second book *Girl Online on Tour*.

Let us closely examine two videos that were recently uploaded by Zoella to gain a better understanding of the microcelebrity practices she follows. During the COVID-19 worldwide lockdown, she posted a video titled "Organising my Bathroom" which showed her going over more than a dozen branded makeup products while rummaging through all the items. The video had been posted on April 30, 2020, and had garnered 787,314 views by June 2020. Zoella had chosen a highly relatable topic since many of us were locked inside our homes during the pandemic and spent time organizing things.

She started the video with a comment that she does remember when she vlogged last. Any viewer would connect with such an observation since time has ceased to have much meaning during the lockdown. As she sorted through the items in her bathroom, she picked a few of those items and read out the brand of the product and its purpose. The topic and style in which the video was made helped her followers connect with her.

It received many comments from her followers. For instance, one of them suggested "Put decorative stuff on the shelves that are too high in your bathroom. You could put like a small vase, a candle, some crystals up there." Another wrote, "I've been sorting through stuff like this too much and now I'm really bored because I have nothing else to sort." The nature of the comments on her video highlights the high engagement between micro-celebrities and their followers.

Zoella posted another video titled "Chilled, chatty mornings & get ready with me" a day before this one. She starts the video with a I-woke-up-just-now look, does her makeup and has her breakfast before getting ready for the day. In this video, Zoella focuses on how lockdown stress has led to her skin breaking out around her chin. Midway through the video, she also comments that hopefully no one has seen the broken zipper on her jeans. She is seen applying hand cream toward the end of her video and struggles to pronounce its French brand name "L'Occitane." Looking at the camera, she wonders if it is the right pronunciation.

Again, one can see how the choice of her topics and nature of presentation make her videos appear realistic and relatable. One of her followers commented, "Love how real you are, not afraid to show who you are and it's so brave." Another wrote, "Looking absolutely stunning even with the broken zipper." Finally, one viewer assures her in a comment that Zoella is pronouncing the French brand right. The video garnered 625,233 views and 386 comments by June 2020.

In the description box located below her videos on YouTube appears the list of products that Zoella uses in her videos and a link to purchase these products. Before the list of products and links appear the following message from Zoella can be seen:

> Links below marked with a "*" are ad-affiliate links – which means I receive a percentage of the revenue made from purchasing products through this link. This does not affect you as the consumer or the price of the product. It is also not a paid for promotion or a collaboration/ advert with the brands featured. Anything featured below may have been sent by PR's, however I am never under any obligation to post & only talk about or use products I like & would naturally recommend.

In an interview with the *Financial Times*, Zoella said that big brands were lining up to cash in on her popularity as she knows how to connect with people in a way that "they can't, even though they've got all the money in the world" (Ford, 2014).

While vloggers may appear to be chatty in their videos, they actually fill as many commonly-searched keywords on their topic as possible into their narrative. They also ensure that they adopt strategic expressions, tone, enunciation, pace, and follow elaborate tagging practices for maximum visibility and impact (Bishop, 2019).

Zoella has been highly effective in promoting beauty products as a part of her personal lifestyle presentation in intimate settings (Berryman & Kavka, 2017). She vlogs from her bedroom and bathroom and "recommends" hundreds of beauty products to millions of followers in a style that one adopts while talking to close friends.

While promoting these products, she makes intimate revelations about her life and relationships. Interestingly, it must be mentioned here that the "bedroom" where Zoella often vlogs is not her own but a spare bedroom in her house that has been "meticulously dressed to imitate a bedroom," a fact that is known to people who regularly view her videos (Berryman & Kavka, 2017, p. 6).

Her day-in-the-life vlogs take audiences behind the scenes. For instance, one of her most watched vlogs titled "I moved house with Alfie" shows both Zoella and Alfie lying in bed together while she declares that they have moved in together. The video has been shot on their first night in the house. It was posted on YouTube on October 14, 2014, and has garnered more than 5.5 million views and 10, 375 comments by June 2020. Many of the commenters on this vlog discuss whether the couple have had sex before vlogging since Alfie is bare-chested in the vlog and Zoella is wearing some loose, strappy clothing while both talk to their cameras from under a comforter. Meanwhile, several people were critical of those who attributed sexual connotations to the vlog.

Commenting on the role of intimacy in promoting products, Richard Berryman and Misha Kavka, both researchers in New Zealand, highlight the intimate setting used in this vlog:

> Alfie's presence in the video makes it clear that we are not simply in bed with Zoe, but in bed with her *and* her boyfriend, which situates us within, and part to, an intimate relationship in its most iconic setting – the bed. (p. 9)

In such vlogs, viewers get to witness how Zoella lives a regular life just like them. She presents herself as the girl-next-door who is just excited about moving in with her boyfriend like any viewer would be in such a situation.

While vlogs are expected to offer glimpses of the private life of vloggers, one must keep in mind that vloggers often choose to share only those snippets of their life that reinforce their brand image and help sell the products that they promote. Such glimpses of their private lives establish a "seamless connection between the ordinary person, the YouTube celebrity, the influencer whom consumers trust, all held together by the behind-the-scenes intimate appeal of the vlogs" (Berryman & Kavka, 2017, p. 10). Zoella's intimacy narrative is very much a part of her brand endorsement strategies.

Moving to a different genre of vlogging, the following section analyzes videos posted by world-famous gamer PewDiePie and the techniques he uses to bond with his "bros."

PewDiePie: Having "fun" at the very edge

PewDiePie is the online persona of Felix Kjellberg, one of the most popular persons on YouTube. Born in 1989 in Sweden, PewDiePie dropped out of university and started uploading videos on YouTube in 2010. At that time, he worked at a hotdog stand and sold his artwork to support himself. While he started his YouTube career doing gaming walkthroughs and reviews, he later expanded to doing satires and meme roundups (Leskin, 2019).

He addresses his viewers as "bros" and not at "fans" seemingly to create a feeling of equality rather than the hierarchy implicit in fandom (Fägersten, 2017). He ends his videos with a "bro fist bump" and a message to his viewers to "stay awesome." PewDiePie has also launched his own video games. Forbes estimated he made $15.5 million in the year 2018 (Leskin, 2019).

Some attribute his success to "goofy charisma and algorithmic luck" (Roose, 2019b). According to Kristy Beers Fägersten, a researcher in Sweden, who examined PewDiePie's interaction style in horror game videos, his intermittent swearing helps to connect and entertain viewers. He re-creates the atmosphere that is characteristic of close friends playing a video game together. Moreover, PewDiePie does not swear at viewers. He swears at the game and at himself. In fact, he swears *in place of* the viewers. While he usually swears in English in his game videos, a translation shows up in the subtitles when he swears in Swedish (Fägersten, 2017).

While Fägersten's arguments about the role of swearing in connecting with people hold true in most cases, it is also a fact that PewDiePie's offensive comments have landed him in much trouble. While people are aware that he frequently jokes online, PewDiePie was briefly removed from Twitter in 2016 for saying that he was joining ISIS (Leskin, 2019).

In 2017, Disney and YouTube both cut ties with him after *Wall Street Journal* reported that some of his videos included "anti-Semitic jokes or Nazi imagery" (Leskin, 2019). In response, PewDiePie released a video attacking the media for trying to discredit him and challenged the media saying "try again mother***er" to take him down. He also got into another major controversy for using a racial slur while livestreaming and for using sexist jokes against female gaming streamers (Leskin, 2019).

While PewDiePie was the most-subscribed-to channel on YouTube since 2013, Indian music network and production house, T-Series, came close to toppling him in 2018. In October 2018, he posted a song criticizing T-Series titled "B***h Lasagna" that mocked the company and referred to stereotypes about Indians (Spangler, 2018). The title "B***h Lasagna" drew upon a meme mocking an Indian man's use of broken English to proposition a woman online (Poonam, 2019). Several of PewDiePie's fans also made many anti-India remarks.

The race continued for months and PewDiePie fans used every medium and method to garner followers for him. Apart from hacking printers, Chromecasts and the *Wall Street Journal*, they even vandalized a World War II–memorial with "Subscribe to PewDiePie" graffiti (Sands, 2019). PewDiePie did not discourage his fans for engaging in such activities. Instead, he framed the competition between him and T-Series as a "Creators vs. Corporations" issue which is as linear and misleading as T-Series framing it as an "India vs. the world" issue (Sands, 2019).

This campaign took a horrifying turn when the gunman who engaged in a mass shooting at a mosque in Christchurch on March 15, 2019, said "Remember lads, subscribe to PewDiePie" before he started his shooting rampage, an event that he livestreamed on Facebook. In response, PewDiePie tweeted that he was "absolutely sickened" having his name taken by the gunman (Roose, 2019a).

Meanwhile, T-Series overtook PewDiePie in March 2019 (Leskin, 2019). On March 31, 2019, PewDiePie posted another diss track titled

"Congratulations" that made fun of the company. This time, T-Series took the matter to court, which ordered YouTube to remove the songs for their "vulgar" and "racist" content ("High Court Orders," 2019).

The "Subscribe to PewDiePie" campaign also ran into problems after PewDiePie uploaded a video on YouTube on April 28, 2019, titled "Ending the Subscribe to Pewdiepie Meme" urging his supporters to stop it. He regretted the fact that what started as a funny thing eventually became so hateful and deadly. Referring to the Christchurch shootings in New Zealand, he said "To have my name associated with something so unspeakably vile has affected me in more ways than I've let shown." The video received a lot of praise from viewers and had been viewed almost 19 million times by June 2020.

In the video, PewDiePie also clarified that he made the diss tracks against T-Series "in fun, ironic jest" and never meant to offend and hurt people of any nationality or race. Emphasizing that the negativity had to stop, he said, "I'm not racist. I don't support any form of racist comments or hate towards anyone."

In an interview with *The New York Times* in October 2019, PewDiePie emphasized that some people mistakenly assume he has white national-ist leanings. Instead, he attributed some of his risk-taking behavior, espe-cially around the year 2015, to a "combination of immaturity, boredom and YouTube's platform incentive" which encouraged creators to behave outra-geously so they can get more people to watch their videos for a longer time (Roose, 2019b).

In fact, some of the controversies made PewDiePie appear like a "mar-tyr" to many of his fans as they believed he was an authentic guy who engaged in straight talk about various issues while others misinterpreted and framed him. But critics believe PewDiePie does not realize the far-reaching nature of his influence and the responsibilities associated with it (Roose, 2019b).

In August 2019, PewDiePie finally reached 100 million subscribers and became the first individual on YouTube to reach that major milestone although T-Series had already reached that mark earlier that year (Webb, 2019). In June 2020, T-Series had 142 million subscribers on YouTube while PewDiePie had 105 million ("Top 100," 2020).

The fact is PewDiePie does an incredible balancing act every single day. As *New York Times* tech columnist, Kevin Roose, argues, PewDiePie has to ensure that he is not so risqué in his videos that he jeopardizes his stand-ing with people who pay him while simultaneously ensuring that he is fun and entertaining to his target audience who view him as a straightforward person with a mind of his own.

For now, it seems PewDiePie wants to stay away from controversies. He has signed an exclusive livestreaming deal with YouTube in the year 2020 and declared that he would be primarily focusing on livestreaming in the future ("PewDiePie signs," 2020).

Let us now explore microcelebrities in India where the number of Internet users rose by 11% between December 2016 and December 2017 largely due to the introduction of cheap data packages (Poonam, 2019). It gave a lot of people in small towns and villages affordable access to the Internet.

Becoming Internet infamous: Lies, lifestyle, and the wellness lore

Internet celebrities may become infamous for the things some of them do in their relentless quest for fame and money. For instance, in 2015, Belle Gibson, an Australian food blogger who had become famous after claiming to have cured brain cancer with diet and lifestyle changes, revealed that she had lied about having cancer after a media company raised doubts about her charity work claims (Khamis et al., 2017). By then, she already had a highly successful blog, a popularly downloaded phone app, and a book deal that would detail her "journey."

Gibson had merely exploited the contemporary trend of attaining "wellness" through diet and lifestyle. Since many today, majority of whom are women, seek health information on the Internet, her strategy of focusing on health and lifestyle fit really well. Her followers believed every word she said. They downloaded her recipes and practiced what she preached. In the preface to her book, *The Whole Panty*, Gibson mentioned her formula for social media popularity as "authenticity and integrity" (Donelly & Toscano, 2015).

But not only had she fabricated her diagnosis of terminal brain cancer, even her claims of giving her profits to charities were found to be fraudulent. Her case shows how Internet celebrities use "compelling narratives" to draw attention to their story and create an attractive persona but truth catches up with them sooner or later (Khamis et al., 2017).

Internet celebrities in India: YouTube and TikTok fight it out

India is home to a highly heterogenous group of YouTubers as it is not restricted to the commonly found "young-male-urban-comedian" variety

(Kadakia, 2018). Thus, it has 59-year-old Nisha Madhulika cooking vegetarian food in a Noida kitchen and 21-year-old Ajey Nagar, who is famous for roasting people on the platform. It also has Dr. Vikram Yadav who is famous for uploading videos on removing blackheads from a person's nose and maggots from another person's scalp. Other top YouTubers in India include Amit Bhadana (comedy), Bhuvan Ban (comedy); Shruti Anand (beauty and lifestyle); Anisha Dixit (women-centric comedy); Tushar Lall (music); Wah chef Sanjay Thumma (food); Ashish Chanchlani (comedy); Gaurav Chaudhary (technology); Himesh Madaan (motivational); Vidya Iyer (music); and Sandeep Maheshwari (motivational), amongst many others.

Videos for children comprise a huge market on YouTube in India and abroad. Top Indian YouTube stars include Anantya Anand, Ajay Sheikh, Samreen Ali, Varchasvi Sharma and Aanya Joshi, amongst others (Balakrishnan, 2019). India is also witnessing the emergence of YouTube families where multiple members of a family are all earning their living on YouTube. Shruti Arjun Anand's family is one such example where 8 members of the family have made YouTube their family business (Dhar, 2017). While three women and a little child host shows on YouTube, four men oversee production and brand endorsements in the Noida-based family.

YouTube has 265 million active monthly users in India and 1,200 Indian channels that have at least a million subscribers (Maji, 2020). It is not only a source of entertainment for many but also a source of educational videos for those who need help covering their syllabus (Poonam, 2019). With growing unemployment, many are also seeking income opportunities on the Internet including on YouTube. Language and regional identity play an important role as far as YouTube viewership in India is concerned. Ninety-five percent of video consumption in India is in local languages (Kakadia, 2018).

TikTok, a popular Chinese video-sharing app owned by Beijing-based Internet technology company, ByteDance, was launched in India in 2017. Today, it is highly popular in the country, especially among audiences in Tier-2 and Tier-3 cities, due its strong artificial intelligence and user-friendly interface (Singh, 2020). TikTok has 120 million active monthly users in India (Mandavia, 2019). India also comprises TikTok's largest market as it accounts for 30% of total downloads of the app (Talukdar, 2020).

Little wonder that TikTok and YouTube have been at war in India. The war between TikTok and YouTube in India has been described as "the new class war on the Internet" and a reflection of the larger debate ranging in the country between "raw aspiration and entrenched entitlement" (Sharma, 2020). Unlike many content creators on YouTube, TikTokers often do not have the resources to shoot in impressive locations, use fancy equipment or invite celebrities to their video shows. In fact, TikTok is considered to be a platform where people from lower socioeconomic sections of society can display their creativity without worrying about financial resources and social capital.

However, TikTok has also been plagued with major controversies and allegations. The Madras High Court briefly banned TikTok on allegations of promoting pornography and exposing children to cybercrime (Bansal, 2020). The company that owns TikTok has been accused of sharing personal information about its users with the Chinese government (Talukdar, 2020). It has also been accused of hosting disturbing content made by its users that normalizes and glorifies sexual violence against women, child abuse, animal abuse, forced religious conversions, etc. The platform has responded by banning thousands of accounts and even partnering with reputed educational institutions to deliver relevant videos (Rawat, 2020).

With anti-Chinese rhetoric spreading in India, especially after the border skirmish in Ladakh in June 2020, will TikTok slide in popularity here? Initially, analysts predicted that the rise of anti-Chinese sentiments was unlikely to end TikTok's popularity in the country even though several public figures requested Indians to stop using Chinese goods and services (Bansal, 2020). Of course, things changed when the Indian government banned 59 Chinese apps including TikTok on June 29, 2020 (Patranobis, 2020).

Now that we have discussed the popularity of various vlogging platforms in India, the following section will examine case studies on Indian Internet celebrities who specialize in different vlogging genres starting with CarryMinati.

CarryMinati: Desi roasts, diss tracks, and skits

Ajey Nagar, who is known as CarryMinati on YouTube, is one of the most popular Indian content creators who posted his first video when he was 10 years old (Jain, 2020). In June 2020, he had 22.4 million subscribers on YouTube. The 21-year-old YouTuber is known for roasting people including celebrities. He livestreams while playing video games on his second YouTube channel, CarryisLive, which has more than 6 million subscribers.

Carry could not take his 12th board examinations as he was nervous about his economics paper. He soon became a full-time YouTuber and completed his high school through distance education. Carry started his YouTube channel in 2014 with videos about football tutorials and moved on to doing mimicry (Jain, 2020).

Today, Carry and his supporting team works out of his Faridabad-based home and makes around 8 videos per month (Poonam, 2019). In 2018, Carry interviewed Tom Cruise and Henry Cavill to help in the promotion of their film *Mission Impossible – Fallout* in India (Kidangoor, 2019). However, Carry always raps in Hindi, which helps him reach a larger audience.

Carry's YouTube career got a major boost when he launched a diss track in response to PewDiePie's "B***h Lasagna" titled "Bye PewDiePie." Here is an excerpt from Carry's track:

Iss Iss Desh Ke Khilaaf Hui Duniya
Kitni Nikaaloge Humari Kamiyan
Aaj Naachega Tu Jaise Chhamiya
Ek Chhamiyan, Ha Han
Khatam Ab Tera Raaj Hua
Peeche Dekh Tera Baap Khada

The video was uploaded on January 1, 2019, and had been viewed more than 36 million times by June 2020. A viewer posted the following comment about the song: "Last time something this hard dropped Japan surrendered." Another one commented: "Imagine hindustani bhau replying to pewdiepie in car."

Using nationalist rhetoric, the song assures Indians that one day their country will rule the world. The lyrics of the song obviously appealed to the patriotic sentiments of Indians. Carry said he wanted the song to motivate Indians to stand up to anyone who mocked their culture and to celebrate their identity instead (Kidangoor, 2019). Carry follows a highly energetic style in his tracks. In 2019, *Time* magazine named him as one of its list of 10 Next Generation Leaders who are carving new paths in different fields (Jain, 2020). CarryMinati has also won several YouTube awards.

In 2020, one of his videos titled "YouTube vs. TikTok: The End" became highly controversial. Carry's video was a response to a video by popular TikTok user Amir Siddiqui who boasted about the camaraderie among TikTok content creators while alleging that YouTubers often plagiarize content from it and instigated YouTubers who roast to respond to his video (Farzeen, 2020).

Carry, who is known as the "Roast King of India" responded by roasting Siddiqui and mocking his grammar slip-ups and the strategies he apparently uses to gain viewer attention (Jain, 2020). After the video gained 70 million views in a week, YouTube removed it for violating terms of service citing the use of homophobic language in the video (India TV Trending Desk, 2020). Carry's fans started a campaign on Twitter with the hashtag #justiceforcarry.

Mumbai-based Amir Siddiqui, who has 3.7 million followers on TikTok, responded with another video saying he was not against YouTube but against the work of specific content creators on it who promoted cyberbullying by roasting people (Farzeen, 2020).

Like PewDiePie's videos, CarryMinati's videos raise many questions about the boundaries of humor on the Internet. Can we normalize laughing about someone else's appearance and/or sexual orientation? Certainly not. How can we preserve freedom of speech and at the same time respect views and values that are radically different from ours? Many of these dilemmas cannot be resolved by framing new laws alone. Internet users need to figure out the boundaries of humor by trial and error.

While the typical YouTuber is young and loud like CarryMinati, there are a few senior citizens who have also made it big on the platform (Dockray, 2018). We will now examine case studies of a few such atypical microcelebrities.

Mastnamma, Grandpa Kitchen, and Nisha Madhulika: Cooking one's way into every viewer's heart

Old age, cataracts, and dentures did not stop Karre Mastanamma from becoming a sensation on YouTube (Schultz, 2018). She lived in a hut made of palm leaves in a small village in Andhra Pradesh. She got married at the age of 11 and her husband died when she was 22. She worked as a laborer to support her five children, four of whom died over the years due to various diseases. But the vagaries of life did not deter her passion for cooking.

In 2016, her great-grandson and his friend started filming her cooking and posting the videos on YouTube (Schultz, 2018). Her traditional recipes became a huge hit on YouTube. One of her most popular dishes is watermelon chicken where she is seen roasting a spicy chicken mix inside a huge watermelon. The video had more than 15 million views in June 2020.

Another video on how to make prawn masala curry had more than 3.5 million views. In this video, she is seen using her bare thumbs to peel ginger and then uses the cup of her palm to toss various spices into the pot. Toward the end of the video, one can see Mastanamma and her family having rice and prawn curry served on one large banana leaf. There were 1,029 comments on this video. The viewers seem to have embraced the simplicity and warmth that Mastanamma showed in her videos.

For instance, a viewer commented: "The end made me cry. So simple and so beautiful." Another viewer commented: "I just discovered this. Reminds me of my Aaji. Thank you so much for sharing yours with us. Love the wind blowing in the background. Just the way my Aaji used to cook outside. Thanks again!!! Bless her with good health."

Mastanamma died a few months after celebrating her 107th birthday in December 2018 (Schultz, 2018). A viewer commented on her funeral video posted on YouTube: "world's cutest grandmaa … 😢 😢 😢 we miss you amma…"

Like Mastnamma, Narayana Reddy, a man in his 70s, cooked on an open fire in the great Indian outdoors. He lived in the outskirts of Hyderabad and cooked both Indian and Western fare—from chicken biryani and Patiala chicken to lasagna, pizza, oreo pudding, KitKat milkshake, KFC style–fried chicken, and more. Interestingly, he cooked dishes such as pizzas and lasagna without an oven. His channel had 7.74 million registered subscribers in June 2020. Although Reddy passed away on October 27, 2019, his family members continue to post videos on his channel.

A *New York Times* report on Reddy's channel pointed out that his videos "followed a straightforward formula: adorable children, heartwarming music, inspirational sayings and seemingly absurd amounts of food" (Slotnik, 2019). Clad in a dhoti and shirt, Reddy cooked especially for orphan children and the poor.

In his videos, Reddy starts with a direct address to the audience "Hello guys! How are you? Welcome to my channel. This is your grandpa." The tagline on his videos says "Loving. Caring. Sharing. This is my family." Reddy's videos earned a lot of praise from viewers from all over the world although a few critical comments were posted as well.

For example, in a video on how to make chicken biryani which had more than 28 million views, a viewer commented "Not very hygienic but whole of India is not." Such comments usually led to a barrage of comments that defended Reddy and his cooking methods. For instance, one viewer wrote, "the wrinkled, black, old hand looks clean, precious and warm to me."

When Reddy died, there was an outpouring of grief from his fans on multiple social media platforms. A viewer left the following comment on his funeral video, "He is not dead he is cooking meals for others in heaven." Another wrote, "A cook was needed in Heaven, RIP Grandpa."

In contrast to Reddy and Mastanamma, Nisha Madhulika, one of India's top 10 YouTubers, has a very urban set up in the suburbs of New Delhi. A media report describes her as "Noida's own Nigella Lawson" (Bhowmick, 2016). Madhulika started her channel in 2011. Her first video showed the world how to make rose water at home. The video generated so much interest that she decided to make more videos on vegetarian fare that is easy to prepare at home.

She started her channel with technical support from her husband. After she became successful, she hired a videographer and set up a separate kitchen studio as well (Bhowmick, 2016). In June 2020, Madhulika's channel had 9.55 million subscribers. She usually shows how to make everyday food on her YouTube channel.

The 59-year-old actively interacts with her fans and promptly replies to several comments posted by her viewers. Her fans also make special requests to her. For instance, a viewer wrote, "I love ur cooking mam.....I would like to see sabudana wada........I have tried it so many times but always they splatter like bombs when I fry them..i don't know where I am going wrong....pls share the recipe...."

Mastanamma, Narayana Reddy, and Nisha Madhulika's success on YouTube highlights the popularity of regional content on the platform. With videos and subtitles, these vloggers reach audiences all over the world. Of course, senior citizens succeeding on YouTube is not just an Indian phenomenon. There are several others who have made it big on the platform. For example, 70-year-old Tricia Cusden teaches how to do makeup to the elderly; Judy Graham gives knitting tips; Grandma Shirley gives gaming tips; and Grandma Lill and her grandson Kevin do comedy (Dockray, 2018). However, what makes Indian seniors' channels unique is the high number of subscribers they manage to garner.

All India Bakchod: When YouTube glory fades away

The case study of the comedy group, All India Bakchod, demonstrates how vloggers can become very famous and disappear from the limelight within a few years. A group of four stand-up comedians, Tanmay Bhat, Gursimran Khamba, Rohan Joshi, and Ashish Shakya founded the YouTube channel in 2013. The title of the channel is a play on the state-run "All India Radio" and the word "Bakchod" is a Hindi slang which refers to someone who engages in idle chatter and gossip. The comedians focused primarily on spoofs and sketches. After becoming an established channel, they often created branded content and promoted various products and services.

The group also used comedy to draw attention to social issues (Pande, 2019). In September 2013, one of their videos titled "Rape: It's your fault" went viral. It featured Bollywood actor, Kalki Koechlin, and highlighted how Indian society often blames women for sexual assaults on them.

Another popular AIB video featured Bollywood actor Alia Bhatt and highlighted her experiences following the highly gendered ridicule and criticism she faced after making an embarrassing mistake while answering a question on a popular television show. AIB roped in other Bollywood actors including Imran Khan and Kangana Ranaut to highlight mainstream Indian attitudes toward male homosexuality and the nepotism and patriarchy prevalent in Bollywood today (Pande, 2019).

By broadly addressing social issues and getting Bollywood actors to join them in several of their videos, AIB managed to occupy a unique brand space where they could commercially benefit from being perceived as dissenting liberals without being dubbed as radical "activists" who may be perceived pejoratively in certain mainstream discourses (Pande, 2019, p. 156).

In the height of its popularity, Tanmay Bhat, co-founder of the channel, was included in the country's list of top 10 YouTube superstars (Goyal, 2016). In 2015, All India Bakchod featured in the Forbes India list of top-earning celebrities (Dixit, 2015). However, their fame and money did not last long. Two of its members, Gursimran Khamba and Tanmay Bhat, were named in the #MeToo movement in India (Singh, 2019b).

In an article titled "How AIB Went From a Rising Star to Having No Money, No CEO and No Office," journalist Nandita Singh describes the fall of the channel even as "the #MeToo movement took AIB from being the country's foremost comedy collective to a group of scattered and apologetic individual players." Of course, their old videos remain on YouTube and the channel still had 3.74 million subscribers in June 2020. However, with no new content being uploaded on the channel, it has definitely slipped from the limelight.

Conclusion

This chapter shows how Internet celebrities from different vlogging genres use a variety of techniques and settings to portray a sense of authenticity and spontaneity that helps them connect with their audiences online. The narrative of intimacy and relatability that they practice also helps to promote various branded products and services as their fans and followers "trust" their recommendations.

With marketers increasingly relying on social media influencers to spread the word on their products and services, even a person with a few thousand followers stands to gain from the trend. Such "nano-influencers" can make a difference because people in their online networks are more likely to believe their suggestions than the company's direct promotions and advertisements (Bhattacharya, 2019).

The case studies in this chapter also highlight how microcelebrities differ in the practices they follow and how much they reveal about their personal lives online. But one thing is clear. It would be wrong to assume that all those who are Internet famous necessarily bare their personal lives online. Instead, privacy for them is an outcome of an individually negotiated process where they actively decide what to reveal, how much to reveal, and when to reveal. Thereby, "authenticity" becomes a calibrated process of revealing some aspects of their lives that buttress their brand image while keeping the rest of it under wraps.

As the number of content creators who want to make money on YouTube and other online platforms keeps increasing, the demand for algorithmic experts who can help them gain visibility is also growing (Bishop, 2020). These experts offer coaching on specific aspects of content creation such as the ideal length for videos, the ideal time of the day to post them on the online platform of their choice, and the most suitable themes to cover in their videos, amongst others. They also offer advice on the most important question that occupies the minds and hearts of every online content creator: What comprises good content?

With the "industrialization" of microcelebrity practices, the differences between traditional celebrities and microcelebrities is likely to get more blurred (Marwick, 2019, p. 164). However, vlogger incomes will also remain vulnerable to algorithmic changes that are often made suddenly, which highlights the "precarity of building a career contingent to platforms" (Bishop, 2020, p. 2).

Despite the uncertainty, many will aspire to make millions on online platforms such as YouTube and opt to become full-timers on it. And social media algorithms will continue to heavily influence what type of content people create and who succeeds in gaining visibility on the Internet.

References

Balakrishnan, R. (2019). Children's day: Meet 5 child YouTubers who are earning lakhs with their videos. Retrieved from https://yourstory.com/herstory/2019/11/childrens-day-five-top-kid-youtubers-india

Baldwin, S. (2004). *Forgotten web celebrities: Jennicam.org's Jennifer Ringley*. Retrieved from https://www.disobey.com/ghostsites/2004_05_19_archive.html

Bansal, S. (2020, June 25). Anti-China narrative is not likely to stop TikTok's rise. *Livemint.com*. Retrieved from https://www.livemint.com/opinion/columns/opinion-anti-china-narrative-is-not-likely-to-stop-tiktok-s-rise-11593048913484.html

Berryman, R., & Kavka, M. (2017). 'I guess a lot of people see me as a big sister or a friend': The role of intimacy in the celebrification of beauty vloggers. *Journal of Gender Studies*, 26(3), 307–320. doi: 10.1080/09589236.2017.1288611

Bhattacharya, A. (2019, January 9). Social media influencers are the latest obsession among India's marketeers. *Quartz India*. Retrieved from https://qz.com/india/1518723/instagram-youtube-stars-are-hot-properties-for-indian-brands/

Bhowmick, S. (2016). 56, and killing it from her kitchen, meet You Tube star Nisha Madhulika, Noida's own Nigella Lawson. *The Times of India*. Retrieved from https://timesofindia.indiatimes.com/city/noida/56-and-killing-it-from-her-kitchen-meet-You-Tube-star-Nisha-Madhulika-Noidas-own-Nigella-Lawson/articleshow/54510864.cms

Bishop, S. (2019). Vlogging parlance: Strategic talking in beauty Vlogs. In C. Abidin & M. L. Brown (Eds.), *Microcelebrity around the globe: Approaches to culture of Internet fame* (pp. 21–32). Bingley, UK: Emerald Publishing.

Bishop, S. (2020). Algorithmic experts: Selling algorithmic lore on YouTube. *Social Media + Society*, 6(1), 1–11. doi: 10.1177/2056305119897323

Dhar, S. (2017, April 23). Meet India's big fat YouTube family. *The Times of India*. Retrieved from https://timesofindia.indiatimes.com/home/sunday-times/meet-i ndias-big-fat-youtube-family/articleshow/58319340.cms

Dixit, M. (2015). AIB features on Forbes India's 2015 list of top-earning celebrities; Tanmay Bhat reacts. *IndiaToday.in*. Retrieved from https://www.indiatoday.in/ lifestyle/what-s-hot/story/aib-debuts-on-forbes-celebrity-100-list-ahead-of-raj nikanth-ss-rajamouli-anupam-kher-276764-2015-12-11

Dockray, H. (2018, November 16). These senior citizen YouTubers are better than anyone else on this hellscape internet. *Mashable.com*. Retrieved from https://ma shable.com/article/senior-citizen-youtubers/

Donelly, B., & Toscano, N. (2015). Supporters turn on Belle Gibson as cancer claims unravel. *The Sydney Morning Herald*. Retrieved from https://www.smh .com.au/technology/supporters-turn-on-belle-gibson-as-cancer-claims-unravel -20150313-1439ny.html

Fägersten, K. B. (2017). The role of swearing in creating an online persona: The case of YouTuber PewDiePie. *Discourse, Context & Media*, *18*, 1–10. doi: 10.1016/j. dcm.2017.04.002, 2211-6958

Farzeen, S. (2020, May 18). CarryMinati's video removed, everything you should know about TikTok vs YouTube controversy. *IndianExpress.com*. Retrieved from https://indianexpress.com/article/entertainment/entertainmen t-others/carryminati-amir-siddiqui-youtube-vs-tiktok 6411239/#:~:text=You Tube%20fans%20have%20been%20left,to%20TikTok%20user%20Amir%20 Siddiqui

Ford, J. (2014). Lunch with FT: Zoella. *Financial Times*. Retrieved from https://ww w.ft.com/content/fa5e47c6-0d9b-11e4-815f-00144feabdc0

Goyal, M. (2016, May 8). Meet India's top 10 YouTube superstars. *The Economic Times*. Retrieved from https://economictimes.indiatimes.com/people/meet-i ndias-top-10-youtube-superstars/meet-indias-youtube-superstars/slideshow/52 173565.cms

Griffin, L. (2019). Zoe Sugg crowned UK's wealthiest female social media star under 30. Retrieved from https://metro.co.uk/2019/10/29/zoe-sugg-crowned-uks -wealthiest-female-social-media-star-aged-30-11002132/

High Court orders YouTube to pull down PewDiePie's 2019 diss tracks against T-Series (2019). *Firstpost.com*. Retrieved from https://www.firstpost.com/tech /news-analysis/high-court-orders-youtube-to-pull-down-pewdiepies-diss-songs -against-t-series-6437621.html

India TV Trending Desk. (2020). Who is Carry Minati and why is he trending on Twitter? Know all about him here. (2020, May 29). Retrieved from https://www .indiatvnews.com/trending/news-who-is-carry-minati-youtube-vs-tiktok-war-6 18561

Jain, A. (2020, June 13). CarryMinati: Everything you should know about the YouTube star. *IndianExpress.com*. Retrieved from https://indianexpress.com/arti cle/entertainment/entertainment-others/everything-you-should-know-about-you tube-star-carryminati-6455510/#:~:text=Ajey%20Nagar%20aka%20CarryM inati%20is,followed%20by%201.7%20million%20users

Jerslev, A. (2016). In the time of the microcelebrity: Celebrification and the Youtuber Zoella. *International Journal of Communication, 10*, 5233–5251.

Kadakia, P. M. (2018, December 13). The motley YouTube stars. *ForbesIndia.com*. Retrieved from https://www.forbesindia.com/article/2018-celebrity-100/the-m otley-youtube-stars/52029/1

Khamis, S., Ang, L., & Welling, R. (2017). Selfbranding, 'micro-celebrity' and the rise of social media influencers. *Celebrity Studies, 8*(2), 191–208. doi: 10.1080/19392397.2016.1218292

Kidangoor, A. (2019, May 16). 'You should be yourself': How a viral You Tube star is embracing his Indian roots. *Time.com*. Retrieved from https://time.com/col lection-post/5584913/carryminati-ajey-nagar-next-generation-leaders/

Krotoski, Aleks (2016, October 18). "Jennicam: The first woman to stream her life on the internet." *BBC News*. Retrieved from https://www.bbc.com/news/magaz ine-37681006

Leskin, P. (2019, September 10). The career of PewDiePie, the controversial 29-year-old who became the first solo YouTuber to reach 100 million subscribers. *BusinessInsider.com*. Retrieved from https://www.businessinsider.in/the-caree r-of-pewdiepie-the-controversial-29-year-old-who-became-the-first-solo-yout uber-to-reach-100-million-subscribers/articleshow/71067389.cms

Maji, N. (2020, January 8). YouTube India: 2020 will see further rise in regional content, gaming. *Businessworld.com*. Retrieved from http://www.businessw orld.in/article/YouTube-India-2020-Will-See-Further-Rise-In-Regional-Content -Gaming/08-01-2020-181715/

Mandavia, M. (2019). Battleground India: TikTok bests Facebook in round 1. *The Economic Times*. Retrieved from https://economictimes.indiatimes.com/tech/internet /battleground-india-tiktok-bests-facebook-in-round-1/articleshow/69316576.cms

Marwick, A. E. (2013). *Status update: Celebrity, publicity, and branding in the social media age*. Yale, CT: Yale University Press.

Marwick, A. E. (2015). Instafame: Luxury selfies in the attention economy. *Public Culture, 27*(1(75)), 137–160. doi: 10.1215/08992363-2798379.

Marwick, A. E. (2019). Epilogue: The algorithmic celebrity: The future of Internet fame and microcelebrity studies. In C. Abidin & M. L. Brown (Eds.), *Microcelebrity around the globe: Approaches to culture of Internet fame* (pp. 161–169). Bingley, UK: Emerald Publishing.

Mavroudis, J. (2019). Fame Labor: A critical autoethnography of Australian digital influencers. In C. Abidin & M. L. Brown (Eds.), *Microcelebrity around the globe: Approaches to culture of Internet fame* (pp. 83–94). Bingley, UK: Emerald Publishing.

Pande, R. (2019). It's just a joke! The payoffs and perils of microcelebrity in India. In C. Abidin & M. L. Brown (Eds.), *Microcelebrity around the globe: Approaches to culture of Internet fame* (pp. 145–160). Bingley, UK: Emerald Publishing.

Patranobis, S. (2020, June 30). India's decision to ban TikTok, WeChat and others becomes trending topic on social media in China. *Hindustan Times*. Retrieved from https://www.hindustantimes.com/india-news/india-s-decision-to-ban-tikt ok-wechat-and-others-becomes-trending-topic-on-social-media-in-china/story- B93EJIndIqmaZp6kexpBiJ.html

PewDiePie signs exclusive live-streaming deal with YouTube. (2020). *BBC.com*. Retrieved from https://www.bbc.com/news/technology-52540437

Poonam, S. (2019, March 14). How India conquered YouTube. *FinancialTimes.com*. Retrieved from https://www.ft.com/content/c0b08a8e-4527-11e9-b168-96a3 7d002cd3

Rawat, A. (2020, May 19). TikTok's popularity in India takes a tumble with back-to-back fiascos. Retrieved from https://inc42.com/buzz/tiktoks-popularity-in-india-takes-a-tumble-with-back-to-back-fiascos/#:~:text=News-,TikTok's%20P opularity%20In%20India%20Takes,With%20Back%2DTo%2DBack%20Fia scos&text=TikTok's%20tryst%20with%20controversy%20seems,media% 20in%20the%20past%20week

Roose, K. (2019a, March 15). A mass murder of, and for, the Internet. *The New York Times*. Retrieved from https://www.nytimes.com/2019/03/15/technology/face book-youtube-christchurch-shooting.html

Roose, K. (2019b, October 9). What Does PewDiePie Really Believe? *The New York Times*. Retrieved from https://www.nytimes.com/interactive/2019/10/09/ magazine/PewDiePie-interview.html

Sands, M. (2019). It's time to unsubscribe from Pewdiepie Vs. T-Series. *Forbes.com*. Retrieved from https://www.forbes.com/sites/masonsands/2019/03/09/its-time-to-unsubscribe-from-pewdiepie-vs-t-series/#2424ed6a3d8a

Schultz, K. (2018). World's oldest celebrity chef, an Indian great-grandma, dies at 107. *The New York Times*. Retrieved from https://www.nytimes.com/2018/12 /06/world/asia/mastanamma-india-chef-dies.html

Senft, T. (2008). *Camgirls: Celebrity and community in the age of social networks*. New York: Peter Lang.

Sharma, U. (2020). TikTok vs YouTube is the new class war on internet. It all began with a roast. *The Print*. Retrieved from https://theprint.in/opinion/pov/tiktok-vs -youtube-is-the-new-class-war-on-internet-it-all-began-with-a-roast/423346/

Singh, A. K. (2020). #YouTube vs. TikTok: Row between CarryMinati-Amir Siddiqui explained. *The Quint*. Retrieved from https://www.thequint.com/tech-and-auto/ tech-news/youtube-vs-tiktok-row-between-carryminati-amir-siddiqui-explained

Singh, D. (2019a, February 10). Millionaires in the making. *Business Today*. Retrieved from https://www.businesstoday.in/magazine/the-hub/millionaires-in -the-making/story/311991.html

Singh, N. (2019b, May 26). How AIB went from a rising star to having no money, no CEO and no office. Retrieved from https://theprint.in/india/how-aib-went-f rom-a-rising-star-to-having-no-money-no-ceo-and-no-office/240976/

Slotnik, D. E. (2019). Narayana Reddy, YouTube Star as 'Grandpa Kitchen,' Has Died. *The New York Times*. Retrieved from https://www.nytimes.com/2019/11 /06/world/asia/grandpa-kitchen-dead.html

Spangler, T. (2018). PewDiePie zooms past 73 million YouTube subscribers as fans rally to keep him ahead of T-Series. Retrieved from https://variety.com/2018/ digital/news/pewdiepie-tseries-youtube-rally-subscribers-73-million-1203078 188/

Talukdar, S. (2020, May 20). TikTok has many issues but banning app for exposing our cultural problems is pointless and counter-productive. *FirstPost.com*.

Retrieved from https://www.firstpost.com/tech/india/tiktok-has-many-issues-but
-banning-app-for-exposing-our-cultural-problems-is-pointless-and-counter-prod
uctive-8388241.html

Taylor, C. (2019, July 19). Kids now dream of being professional YouTubers rather than
astronauts, study finds. *CNBC.com*. Retrieved from https://www.cnbc.com/2019/07
/19/more-children-dream-of-being-youtubers-than-astronauts-lego-says.html

Top 100 subscribed YouTube channels (sorted by subscriber count). *SocialBlade
.com*. Retrieved from https://socialblade.com/youtube/top/100/mostsubscribed

Webb, K. (2019, August 26). PewDiePie just became the first solo YouTuber to
reach 100 million subscribers. *BusinessInsider.com*. Retrieved from https://www
.businessinsider.in/small-business/tech/pewdiepie-just-became-the-first-solo-yo
utuber-to-reach-100-million-subscribers/articleshow/70845282.cms

5   Digital activism

The power of hashtags and memes

Digital activism is an effective way of garnering extensive support for spe-cific causes. A spontaneous tweet, a blog post, or a short video clip posted by an individual on social media can start a cascade of responses that grow into a powerful campaign in no time. Corporates can neglect such activism at their own peril as it can not only damage their hard-earned reputations but their finances as well. The situation is no different for governments. A government body that turns a blind eye to an online movement will bear the consequences of such indifference even as the online momentum spills into offline spaces in the form of protests on the streets, marches, and demonstrations.

Even when a digital campaign does not immediately result in street pro-tests, it can have a massive impact by highlighting an existing problem. The #MeToo campaign is a good example. Here are a few questions for you. When does complimenting a colleague's outfit slip into the category of sexual harassment? Is sharing sexual jokes at the workplace acceptable? Where does one draw the line between acceptable behavior at the work-place and sexual harassment? What can a person facing harassment at the workplace do to protect herself? How can a firm render the workplace safe? These are some of the questions corporate India grappled with after the #MeToo movement started in India following Bollywood actor Tanushree Dutta's accusation of sexual harassment against veteran actor Nana Patekar in 2018 (Bhushan, 2018).

The #MeToo campaign was originally started by sexual harassment sur-vivor and activist Tarana Burke in 2006 to "show the world how widespread and pervasive sexual violence is" and "to let other survivors know they are not alone" (Ohlheiser, 2017). However, the #MeToo campaign gained wide-spread support only in 2017 when American actor Alyssa Milano, following the revelations about American film producer Harvey Weinstein, posted a tweet on October 16, 2017, asking all women who have been sexually har-assed to write "'Me too" as a reply to the following tweet: "If all the women who have been sexually harassed or assaulted wrote 'Me too' as a status, we might give people a sense of the magnitude of the problem" (Khomami, 2017). Millions of women across the world responded with accounts of sexual harassment that they had faced and the #MeToo hashtag took Twitter by storm. The #MeToo campaign is considered one of the most successful instances of digital activism.

Here, it's important to keep in mind that online activism or digital activism is a generic term used to refer to a variety of online behavior. According to Encyclopaedia Britannica, digital activism is a "form of activism that uses the Internet and digital media as key platforms for mass mobilization and political action" (Fuentes, n.d.). The term may broadly refer to the use of digital technology for political purposes or more specifically to forms of hacktivism, denial of service attacks, and hashtag activism, amongst others (Kaun & Uldam, 2018). We need to keep these varied meanings of digital activism in mind while exploring related practices in different parts of the world.

We should also avoid overemphasizing the technological aspects of digital activism while ignoring the sociopolitical and cultural contexts in which digital practices are situated as both influence one another (Kaun & Uldam, 2018). We need to engage with the digital activism ecosystem rather than focusing on the development of any particular social media platform or mobile device (Kaun & Uldam, 2018). This chapter attempts such an exercise by analyzing the roots of digital activism and critical moments in the journey. It starts with a brief timeline of the development of digital activism in India and the world. The defining characteristics of digital activism are identified after examining critical aspects of hashtag campaigns, memes, and short videos. A discussion on the limits of digital activism follows.

Let us start with the case of India. Digital activism grew roots in India during the Anti-Corruption Movement led by Anna Hazare in 2011 and the Delhi Gang Rape protests in 2012 (Mishra, 2019). During both these protests, people used social media to spread their message and announce venues for people to gather and the timings of such events. Journalists also used social media to both follow and report events associated with the protest.

In the early years, social media forums primarily reflected opinions of the English-speaking, urban middle class. However, the usage of social media gradually spread to India's towns and villages and Indian-language posts started becoming more visible with the increasing availability of Indian-language-enabled mobile phones and cheap data packages.

Specific events also gave a boost to the use of Indian languages on social media forums. For instance, use of Indian languages on Facebook received a boost during the pro-Jallikattu protests in the southern state of Tamil Nadu in January 2017 (Mishra, 2019). Facebook posts were used to organize protests even as thousands opposed the Supreme Court ruling that banned Jallikattu, which is a popular bull-taming sport in Tamil Nadu, after a case was filed by an animal-rights group, PETA (People for the Ethical Treatment of Animals). Following the protests, the Tamil Nadu government passed a bill that exempted the application of the Prevention of Cruelty to Animals Act to Jallikattu making it a legal sport in the state during specific months (Sivakumar, 2017).

Taberez Neyazi, a communications and new media scholar, uses the term "Internet vernacularization" to describe the massive growth in online vernacular content and the growing number of people accessing such content from urban and rural areas in India. The number of Indian-language Internet users has been growing steadily in the country. More specifically, while the number of Indian-language Internet users was about 234 million in 2016, it is projected to reach 536 million in 2021. Meanwhile, the number of English-language Internet users in India which amounted to about 175 million in 2016 is projected to increase to 199 million in 2021(Diwanji, 2019). While "Internet vernacularization" has helped include more Indians in digital spaces, it has also led to challenges, which we will discuss later in the chapter.

In order to understand the complex nature of digital activism, we must start with examining the pillars upon which it stands. With this goal in mind, let us explore the nature of hashtag campaigns, memes, and viral video clips in the following pages.

Hashtag activism

Hashtags involve adding a # sign to a word or phrase while posting on a social media platform, especially Twitter, with the purpose of grouping messages associated with a specific issue or topic. Former Google developer, Chris Messina, conceived of hashtags to "organize information and conversations" on Twitter (Couts, 2015). This makes it easier for users to find a particular conversation by searching for the associated hashtag online. Hashtags help spread information fast and bring like-minded people together. Broadly, hashtag activism refers to Internet users supporting a cause online with a like, share, or tweet. A specific hashtag may become highly popular by gaining online traction and leading to offline protest-related activities such as rallies and flash mobs.

The birth of hashtag activism can be traced to the Occupy Wall Street protests in the United States in 2011. The protests started on September 17, 2011, in Liberty Square in Manhattan's financial district and soon spread to other cities in the United States. Pioneers of the movement described the movement in the following words on the OccupyWallSt.org website:

> [Occupy Wall Street] #ows is fighting back against the corrosive power of major banks and multinational corporations over the democratic process, and the role of Wall Street in creating an economic collapse that has caused the greatest recession in generations. The movement is inspired by popular uprisings in Egypt and Tunisia, and aims to fight back against the richest 1% of people that are writing the rules of an unfair global economy that is foreclosing on our future.

Micah White, one of the pioneers of the movement who was a senior editor with Vancouver-based anti-consumerist magazine *Adbusters* first published a call to action against the growing influence of corporate forces ("About," 2011). The magazine, which has a long history of publishing shocking images that help to rally people around an issue, used the picture of a ballerina perched on a raging bull with people in gas masks behind it as a dominant visual for the movement (Beeston, 2011). The poster carried the message "#occupywallstreet" on it and mentioned the date on which people were expected to gather on Wall Street along with an instruction to bring a tent.

Meanwhile, the "We are 99%" project was launched on Tumblr, an American microblogging platform, to promote the movement. The slogan "We are 99%" refers to the prevailing economic inequalities in the United States between the richest 1% of the population and the rest of the people. The project involved getting ordinary people to post their pictures holding a hand-written poster that explained the specific impact of harsh financial times on their lives (Weinstein, 2011). Their hand-written accounts resonated with a lot of people as they offered personal stories of the economic hardships they were facing and the hard choices they had made to survive them. Soon, thousands of people started posting on the blog and "We are 99%" became the slogan of the movement. One of the defining characteristics of the movement was its decentralized and participatory nature (Berrett, 2011), which was visible both in offline and online spaces.

Analysis of the Occupy Wall Street movement shows how digital campaigns gather momentum when people share hard-hitting personal accounts of their own experiences. These accounts create a sense of authenticity and urgency which helps in persuading others to join the cause. After #OWS came #StopSOPA which channelized anger against the Stop Online Piracy Act. When the bill failed in early 2012, it became evident that online activism could have actual consequences (Couts, 2015). The #Kony2012 campaign which marked the widespread popularity of a 2012 American documentary demanding the arrest of Ugandan militia leader Joseph Kony by the end of that year, contributed to the decision by the African Union and the United States to send troops to Uganda (Couts, 2015).

The #IceBucketChallenge and #BlackLivesMatter movements were two other highly successful hashtag campaigns. The #IceBucketChallenge involved people recording themselves while dumping a bucket of ice water on their heads and posting it on social media forums with the goal of spreading awareness and raising funds to fight ALS (Amyotrophic Lateral Sclerosis), a neurological disease characterized by the death of neurons that control voluntary muscle movement (National Institute of Neurological Disorders and Stroke, n.d.).

In 2013, the #BlackLivesMatter movement grew out of an emotional Facebook post by Alicia Garza on the acquittal of George Zimmerman, a neighborhood watch volunteer in Florida who shot dead a 17-year-old unarmed African American boy called Trayvon Martin when he was returning from a convenience store with iced tea and candy, in February 2012 (Day, 2015). Seeing the response to her post, Garza and two other activists then set up Tumblr and Twitter accounts and encouraged users to share their stories on the issue using the hashtag #BlackLivesMatter (Day, 2015).

The movement grew in strength after another unarmed African American teen, Michael Brown, was shot dead by a white police officer in Ferguson, Missouri (Day, 2015). While protesting police brutality against African Americans on the streets of various American cities and towns, supporters of the campaign carried banners using the same hashtag. In fact, the hashtag became so popular that people began using T-shirts, hats, mugs and badges with #BlackLivesMatter mentioned on them. An Xiao Mina (2019), a Harvard University researcher who has done extensive work on online movements, points out that the #BlackLivesMatter movement was one of the initial campaigns that showed how hashtags from the online world can transfer to the physical world. Today, there are several #BlackLivesMatter chapters across the United States.

Commenting on the nature of the #BlackLivesMatter movement, journalist Elizabeth Day wrote in *The Guardian* newspaper:

> The new movement is powerful yet diffuse, linked not by physical closeness or even necessarily by political consensus, but by the mobilising force of social media. A hashtag on Twitter can link the disparate fates of unarmed black men shot down by white police in a way that transcends geographical boundaries and time zones. A shared post on Facebook can organise a protest in a matter of minutes. Documentary photos and videos can be distributed on Tumblr pages and Periscope feeds, through Instagrams and Vines. Power lies in a single image. Previously unseen events become unignorable.

After the success of these early hashtag campaigns, it became an established fact that tweets, links, and shares carry the potential to shake things in the real world if they gathered the required momentum and could be sustained over a period (Couts, 2015). Several hashtag movements have helped people to talk back to power, to reverse the gaze, and break the silence on specific issues.

However, it must also be noted that a popular hashtag in a country may not have anything to do with supporting a cause. It may be about entertainment or sports. For instance, according to Twitter data, the top five hashtags in India in the first half of 2019 were #Viswasam (a Tamil film); #LokSabhaElections2019 (Parliamentary Elections 2019); #CWC19 (Cricket World Cup); #Maharishi (Telugu film); and #NewProfilePic #HashtagDay (People tweeting about updating their profile pictures).

Apart from hashtag campaigns which help in bringing like-minded people together in support of an issue, memes offer a great way to build popular support for an issue. Let us analyze the nature of memes and the role they play in digital cultures.

Memes

An Internet meme usually comprises an image or clip embedded with text or audio that draws attention to human behavior in a humorous way (Gil, 2020). The word "meme" was first introduced by evolutionary biologist Richard Dawkins in 1976 and originates from the Greek word "mimema" meaning "something imitated" (Gil, 2020). Internet memes help grab attention of ordinary people as they combine pop culture with serious political and social issues (Mina, 2019). An Xiao Mina (2019), author of the book *Memes to Movements*, refers to memes as "street art" of the Web due to their "varied, expressive, and complex" nature (p.12).

Memes use ordinary images and symbols to start a conversation. This explains why so many memes use images of animals such as cats and dogs even when they are referring to serious political and social issues. Mina (2019) argues that one should not dismiss these animal memes as "low culture" as the act of creating memes transforms an Internet user from a consumer to a content producer. Moreover, memes are often the first step in a series of actions an individual might take to express his or her opinion on an issue. Further, the very process of creating and sharing memes is a social process. It is not an isolated act as users continually remix and repurpose them to reflect their own beliefs and interests.

Since memes are participatory in nature and draw upon humorous visuals and catchy hashtags and phrases, it becomes easier to grab the attention of many people online. Visuals stay in our minds longer than just text. Memes frame issues in specific ways and give birth to narratives around them even as the message embedded in them gets repeated over time by a multiplicity of users (Mina, 2019). People from all over the world like, comment, and post the same hashtag and meme creating online momentum on an issue. Memes can also challenge established narratives and introduce new frameworks on an issue.

Creating memes has also become a lucrative activity. India has witnessed the rise of the meme economy in the past few years with consumer brands increasingly using them as a marketing tool to engage with users and stay trendy (Kar, 2020). Earlier, meme pages relied primarily on Google advertisements, videos, or cross-promotions for revenue. Today, they make anywhere between Rs. 10 lakh and Rs. 6 crore in yearly turnover (Kar, 2020).

In India, memes often use songs, dialogues, and scenes from popular Bollywood movies to make a point. It was no different after the COVID-19 outbreak in January 2020. For instance, to spread the message on precautions against COVID-19, Bollywood actor Kajol used the iconic train scene from the classic film "Dilwale Dulhaniya Le Jayenge" where Simran's father lets her run to catch the train and Raj is standing at the compartment door with an outstretched hand to help her get on. The image was edited to place a hand sanitizer in Kajol'shands and the text read "Even Simran knows the importance of sanitizing" ("Kajol shares," 2020). Similarly, another popular meme used the character of gangster Ganesh Gaitonde in the Indian Web television series "Sacred Games" to make a point about COVID-19. An image of Lifebuoy's "Immunity Boosting Sanitizer" replaced Gaitonde's face in the meme and the accompanying text read "Kabhi Kabhi lagta hai apun hi Bhagwan hai" [Sometimes I feel I am God] with the hashtags "#coronavirus India" and "#coronaalert" (Trends Desk, 2020).

Furthermore, in countries characterized by heavy censorship and surveillance, such as China, memes acquire an even greater role. Mina (2019) explains the Chinese context:

> In the case of authoritarian governments, memes reflect the work of highly digitally literate bodies that seek to leverage the power of memes to spread a unified message or create enough confusion to tamp down attention on a message they don't like. (p. 186)

Take the case of the popular "Cao Ni Ma" meme, which literally translates to "grass mud horse" and is a play on a profanity in the Mandarin language. The meme shows the image of an alpaca-like animal and became popular as a method of opposing Internet censorship in China by ridiculing and challenging the government's surveillance projects without referring to them overtly. A *New York Times* article titled "A Dirty Pun Tweaks China's Online Censors" explains the phenomenon:

So while "grass-mud horse" sounds like a nasty curse in Chinese, its written Chinese characters are completely different, and its meaning— taken literally—is benign. Thus the beast not only has dodged censors' computers, but has also eluded the government's own ban on so-called offensive behavior. (Wines, 2009)

The popularity of the "grass mud horse" meme in China shows how memes as a product of digital activism can "evade censorship in a tactical way, by shifting and morphing to avoid keyword-search algorithms or by avoiding words altogether, using the power of in-jokes to avoid censors' scrutiny" (Mina, 2019, p. 46).

Now that we have discussed hashtags and memes, let us take a look at another form of digital activism that is sweeping the world. It involves using short video clips to highlight an issue.

Video activism: Short clips strive for social change

Today, our first reaction when we see something wrong happening in front of us is to record it using our cellphones and post it on social media with a brief description and a catchy hashtag apart from forwarding it to everyone on our personal online networks. Video activism on social media platforms such as YouTube, Facebook, WhatsApp, Twitter, Snapchat, Instagram, and more recently TikTok have become a part of our everyday lives. We believe that visuals offer proof that the incident occurred and the potential for deep engagement as well.

In fact, many believe that TikTok, the Chinese video-sharing app that allows users to create and post videos under 60 seconds, has become the "go-to app for political activism" for Generation Z, that is people born between mid-1990s and 2010s (Borissova, 2019). Videos highlighting political and social causes abound on the platform. For instance, videos highlighting low pay for teachers, terrible side-effects of cancer treatment, discrimination against LGBT communities, awareness videos on aboriginal culture, climate change, etc., can be found on the platform (Price, 2019). Users claim that it is the "lighthearted" nature of the app that helps in popu- larizing videos on social causes and enables users "to be activists without feeling the full weight of activism" (Price, 2019).

Some people are also using TikTok videos to spread a political message while escaping state surveillance as evident in the case of Afghan-American teenager Feroza Aziz's makeup tutorial video posted on the platform. The video starts with Aziz instructing viewers how to curl their eyelashes and suddenly goes on to discussing the plight of Muslims in Chinese internment camps (Kuo, 2019). Aziz talks about Muslims being kidnapped, raped, and murdered in these camps while continuing to show viewers how to curl their eyelashes (Kuo, 2019). Unless someone heard the voiceover in the entire video, it would be difficult to decipher its true intent by just looking at a teenager curling her eyelashes.

Of course, videos on social and political causes are not the only content on the platform as short videos on jokes, dance trends, music, etc., remain dominant. Since the platform has a video-only interface, it has a low entry barrier that makes it popular across social strata (Varadhan & Kalra, 2019). TikTok is highly popular among teenagers in India including those in rural areas. Responding to a PIL in April 2019, the Madras High Court asked the Indian government to ban the app for "encouraging pornography" and prohibit its downloads (Varadhan & Kalra, 2019). Since the app is very popular with children, the court claimed that it exposes them to pedophiles. However, after the company claimed to remove millions of videos that violated its "terms of use and community guidelines" and filed a plea in court (Chandrashekhar, 2019), the ban was lifted.

Let us now look at the characteristics that are common to the various avatars of digital activism we have discussed.

Defining features of digital activism

Digital activism facilitates interlinkages between local and global events and narratives

A movement on social media can link disparate events under one umbrella or one powerful hashtag. For instance, the #BlackLivesMatter movement has highlighted several other cases of police brutality against African American men and women apart from the cases of Trayvon Martin and Michael Brown. It has also inspired similar movements across the world such as the #DalitLivesMatter movement in India.

When Rohith Vermula, a Dalit doctoral student at the University of Hyderabad committed suicide on January 17, 2016, protests ensued in many places across India alleging caste-based discrimination on university campuses (Thakur, 2019). While the word "Dalit" implies "oppressed" people, the administrative terminology used in India for the term is "scheduled castes" (Thakur, 2019). However, "Dalit" is a heterogenous term that may be used to refer to people from different regions, faiths, class, political affiliations, etc. According to the 2011 Indian census, Dalits comprise a large community of more than 200 million people (Thakur, 2019).

Many of the protests following Vermula's tragic suicide were led by Dalit activists and leaders who used social media platforms to coordinate their efforts and mobilize people. Online spaces provided a new avenue for expression of Dalit causes as they no longer had to depend on legacy media alone to highlight their grievances and demands. Drawing inspiration from the terminology used in the #BlackLivesMatter movement in the United States, the online campaign, #DalitLivesMatter, started on Twitter (Thakur, 2019).

Dalit activists used both offline and online techniques combining online petitions, tweets, and blogs with demonstrations and marches to create the necessary momentum (Thakur, 2019). Importantly, although the #DalitLivesMatter campaign emerged as a response to Rohith Vermula's suicide, it served as a rallying point for similar atrocities against the Dalit community. Activists from the #DalitLivesMatter campaign and those from the #BlackLivesMatter campaign drew inspiration from one another. Arvind Thakur (2019), a New Delhi–based researcher, describes this phenomenon well:

> Despite the differences in the lived experiences of Trayvon Martin, Michael Brown, and Rohith Vemula, online articulations are drawing connections and shared symbolism. As illustrated by the Vemula agitation, transnational connections have brought a new reach and resonance for global agitations. (p. 8)

Similarly, the Occupy movements in the West inspired Occupy movements in other parts of the world including Hongkong in 2013 where #occupycentralwithloveandpeace started with the goal of resisting Beijing's growing influence on the city (Mina, 2019). Apart from linking disparate events, online movements also help to illuminate issues that suffer from social stigma.

Digital activism can make the socially stigmatized visible and acceptable in the public domain:

Digital activism has helped make socially shunned issues visible by catapulting them into public spaces where everyone can share their experiences. The #MeToo movement stands out as an important example in this regard. The #MeToo campaign went beyond focusing on the misdeeds of one man and introduced a discussion about men's behavior toward women across the world (Khomami, 2017). More people began to acknowledge that amongst those who sexually harassed women were seemingly "good guys" who had wives and children at home; who were skilled and successful in their professions; and who even supported social causes (Khomami, 2017). The campaign also led to the rise of "whisper networks" among women which were used to warn others about men who habitually engaged in sexual harassment (Khomami, 2017).

During the #MeToo movement in India, women named their alleged abusers, many of whom held powerful positions in Bollywood, politics, and the news media (Jain, 2020). Corporate India responded with sensitization workshops and anti-harassment training for employees. Many brainstormed on how to create fair and inclusive workplaces where there is no retaliation against a complainant (Bhushan, 2018). Hushed conversations about sexual harassment in the workplace began to be replaced by robust discussions in public spaces as it was no longer a taboo to bring up the topic (Bhattacharya & Dasgupta, 2018).

However, many Indian women who called out their alleged abusers also faced a social backlash as they were labeled as "trouble makers" and accused with apparently destroying men's careers without any basis (Jain, 2020). They were also accused for merely seeking publicity on flimsy grounds. Jhalak Jain, who writes on intersectional feminism, argues that despite the backlash, the #MeToo movement in India represented a landmark moment:

> It began an open conversation about what inappropriate behaviour and harassment constitute. It forced companies and institutions to introspect, constitute Internal Complaints Committee (ICC) and follow the Sexual Harassment of Women at Workplace (Prevention, Prohibition and Redressal) Act, 2013, also known as POSH law.

The future will show whether corporate India will take cases of sexual harassment seriously after the #MeToo campaign loses momentum (Bhattacharya & Dasgupta, 2018).

Digital activism requires sustained effort by multiple stakeholders to bring about policy change

While it may appear that digital movements including hashtag campaigns and memes succeed without any centralized leadership, a deeper probe would show how specific organizations contribute to the spread of each campaign (Couts, 2015). In fact, an important aspect of hashtag activism comprises multipronged efforts by organized and unorganized actors to keep the issue in the public eye for a sustained period, both online and offline. For instance, an Indian feminist nonprofit organization SheSays introduced a campaign #LahukaLagaan (which means "tax on blood") to protest against the government's decision to impose 14% Goods and Services Tax (GST) on sanitary pads by categorizing them as luxury products (Fadnis, 2017).

Apart from suitable tweets, the organization posted a parody video by a popular feminist comedian that resonated with the audiences (Fadnis, 2017). The organization also filed a petition in the High Court demanding judicial intervention. Meanwhile, celebrities and public figures joined the cause on Twitter along with ordinary citizens urging the government to make sanitary pads tax-free (Fadnis, 2017). Legacy media, both at the national and international levels, also took up the cause. The supporters of the campaign highlighted how girls could not go to school during their period as they did not have access to feminine hygiene products, which also created health hazards (Banerji, 2018). They also drew attention to the irony that sanitary pads were being taxed as a luxury product while condoms were tax-free (Banerji, 2019).

Initially, the government responded by reducing the tax from 14% to 12%. But the campaign continued and the combined efforts of multiple actors on multiple forums, offline and online, led to the Indian government finally dropping taxes on sanitary pads in July 2018 (Banerji, 2018). Deepa Fadnis, a researcher at the University of Texas at Austin, explains:

> What started as a hashtag on Twitter soon turned into a multimodal digital campaign that utilized every possible social media platform to spread the message. People used creative modes of protest to disseminate new modes of discourse through memes, GIFs, profile pictures, personal account videos and status messages to show their solidarity for the cause. (p. 1112)

This example shows how digital activism does not bring about policy changes overnight but requires sustained efforts by multiple stakeholders.

Elizabeth Losh, digital culture scholar at the University of California, examined the "hashtag activist labor" that activist groups often engage in to introduce and promote campaigns online. She highlighted the tremendous effort that activists put into managing metadata and sharing relevant links, audio, video, and more with the target audiences online:

> Choosing, using, and appropriating online hashtags can require significant expenditures of labor. Lengthy periods of work and repetitive activities can be taxing, as can time-intensive design processes of iteration, reflection, deliberation, and discussion with other human rights knowledge workers to refine hashtag use....Hashtags must be simultaneously short, unique, memorable, unambiguous in meaning, resistant to variant spellings, and descriptive as content labels. (Losh, 2014, p. 20)

While digital activism can move mountains by bringing people together to support an issue, it also suffers from certain limitations.

Limits of digital activism

May reinforce regressive and deeply conservative voices

Social media forums have made movements more "complicated and open-ended" (Mina, 2019, p. 4). While these forums offer spaces where people can use their creativity to energize movements and make them more inclusive, they also provide an avenue for expression of hate and extreme beliefs. In online spaces, power can be both reinforced, on the one hand, and challenged by those at the margins of society, on the other.

Hashtags and memes can help spread misinformation and propaganda that reflect strong ideological viewpoints and allegiances of its creators. For instance, people with extreme opinions can use memes to introduce their ideas into mainstream public discourse and expand the borders of what is considered acceptable (Mina, 2019). Memes with opposing messages create contests and contradictions in online spaces even as they strive to recruit as many people as possible for their cause. Such contestations can exacerbate existing social tensions. However, Mina (2019) argues that hashtags and memes per se cannot be blamed for polarizing people as they draw upon existing social beliefs.

Scholars have drawn attention to the "conflicting faces of digital politics" in India and elsewhere which includes new forms of participation and self-expression, on the one hand, and mob vigilantism resulting from widespread circulation of misinformation and provocative visuals, on the other (Udupa, Venkataraman & Khan, 2020). While digital media have facilitated organized political expression among ordinary people, they have also facilitated the spread of propaganda by established political actors. Moreover, with Indians posting on social media forums in so many languages, it's difficult to filter controversial, misleading, and provocative content (Neyazi, 2019).

WhatsApp, a platform used by around 400 million Indians (Hashmi, 2020) has become a major source for the spread of rumors and fake news. Alia Allana (2017) explains:

> The gifts of free usage and anonymity have made WhatsApp the most popular tool to spread both outlandish stories and politically motivated rumors….WhatsApp has been turned into the primary messenger of prejudice, delivering relentless virtual fuel to keep the embers of modern hatreds alive.

Digital practices in India are also influenced by politics of caste, religion, community, region, and class (Udupa, Venkataraman & Khan, 2020). In fact, digital media offer new ways of organizing around old affiliations such as religion, caste, and community.

May not be democratic and egalitarian spaces

Since the social divisions and inequalities of the real world are also reflected online, not all voices get ready access or equal representation online (Dey, 2020). For instance, while India had as many as 688 million active Internet users in January 2020 (Diwanji, 2020), various types of digital divides can be identified. A person's location, income, gender, education, language, and age influence whether a person has access to the Internet (Parsheera, 2019). While the Internet density in urban areas is 97.9%, it's only 25.3% in rural areas where 66% of the country's population lives (Parsheera, 2019). Only 16% of Indian women use mobile and internet services, according to a 2019 report by the GSMA, a body which represents mobile operators worldwide (Parsheera, 2019).

Digital platforms facilitate the expression of individual and collective dissent. However, one needs to keep in mind that these alternative spaces where counter-discourses are formulated and distributed widely may not be accessible to all (Dey, 2020). In this context, Adrija Dey, a gender studies scholar, draws upon American critical theorist Nancy Fraser's concept of "subaltern counterpublics" comprising marginalized people who rarely get a chance to voice their views in mainstream spaces, and emphasizes its flawed and fractured nature:

> The subaltern counterpublics are not always democratic, egalitarian, and virtuous spaces, and even if they are, they are not always above practicing their own exclusions and marginalization. (Dey, 2020, p. 1437)

This explains why fissures develop even when social media and the Internet help to rally people around a cause. In case of the #DalitLivesMatter campaign, multiple narratives existed within the movement as it was characterized by a range of political positions and affiliations that limited the scope of collective action (Thakur, 2019). Hence, it is important to remind ourselves that social media platforms do not just bring diverse forces together in the quest of a common cause; they can also serve to highlight differences in their views and beliefs.

May promote laziness and "slacktivism"

Internet activism has been criticized as a form of "slacktivism," which is a portmanteau of slacker and activism, as it is perceived by many as merely enhancing the "feel-good factor" for participants and having little real-life impact (Christensen, 2011). Would you agree? Does hashtag activism really reflect laziness amongst people? Do people like, share, or tweet about a cause as an effort in personal branding? Or are they committed to the cause in the long run? Answers to such questions can never be simple.

In this context, American columnist and author David Carr commented:

> In the friction-free atmosphere of the Internet, it costs nothing more than a flick of the mouse to register concern about the casualties of far-flung conflicts. Certainly, some people are taking up the causes that come out the Web's fire hose, but others are most likely doing no more than burnishing their digital avatars.

In an article debating whether posting on social media is a valid form of activism, James B Bailey, professor at George Washington University, pointed out:

> Social media is just plain ironic. One the one hand, it has unparalleled reach, making it tailor-made for activism. On the other hand, anyone can express themselves, without expertise, temperament or even conviction. (Suciu, 2019)

Despite the criticism, political science scholar Henrik Serup Christensen, who studies impact of the Internet on political participation, argues that as the Internet helps mobilize people offline as well, there is little evidence today of digital activism being inconsequential and lazy. Then again, the fact remains that while a video or tweet can become viral in very little time, it can also be replaced easily by the next trending message making it difficult to maintain online visibility for a sustained period.

Furthermore, tweets, hashtags, and memes can rarely explore the complexity and nuanced nature of a sociopolitical issue. The need for spontaneity and speed can kill context and the practice of verification amongst journalists (Mishra, 2019). Since it's important to post powerful visuals to get attention on social media, the focus may shift toward capturing shocking visuals rather than in-depth analyses.

Conclusion

This chapter has emphasized the importance of understanding the socio-cultural and political roots of an online campaign instead of focusing on its technological aspects alone. Touching upon varied forms of digital activism, it has highlighted the defining characteristics of the phenomenon. One of the most important aspects of digital activism includes its ability to link disparate events together, both at the local and global levels, under one powerful hashtag. While the seeds of a digital movement may have been planted by a spontaneous tweet or post, it takes sustained labor by activists to acquire critical mass and bring about policy change. Furthermore, hashtag campaigns and memes can catapult socially stigmatized issues into mainstream public spaces thereby making them more visible and acceptable.

Successful digital campaigns carry lessons for marketing professionals. Analysis of such campaigns shows that authentic issues that resonate with people accompanied by catchy hashtags and short and impactful videos help grab attention. Keeping the entry barrier low for someone who wants to participate in the campaign can also go a long way in ensuring the success of a campaign. While it's easier for nonprofits to champion a cause rather than for a commercial entity, several brands have been successful in incorporating social causes into their marketing mix. However, such an effort needs to be genuine and relatable to its target audience and should not be perceived solely as an attempt to increase profits ("Ice bucket challenge," 2014).

The limitations of hashtag campaigns and memes also need to be kept in mind. It is very difficult to sustain an issue online and continue to attract media attention over a long period. A topic that is trending on a social media forum today may disappear tomorrow. An online campaign stands the risk of being hijacked by conservative forces that spread hate and misinformation. Despite the limitations, one needs to acknowledge the primary contribution of online activism: Hashtag campaigns and memes help to garner attention and shape narratives on an emerging issue (Mina, 2019). Narratives, in turn, shape the contours of normative behavior and what is considered acceptable in a society.

Narratives on social media also influence the agenda of traditional news media such as television and newspaper outlets (Mina, 2019). Editors of traditional news media outlets constantly scan social media forums, especially Twitter, for breaking news. Politicians, business leaders, sportspersons, Bollywood actors, and public figures often make important announcements on Twitter. Then again, journalists also post their reports on social media forums and explore new story ideas in the comments posted by users. Since social media and traditional media have become highly complementary in nature, one of the ways in which the professional capital of a journalist is measured today is by the number of followers he or she has on social media forums, especially Twitter (Mishra, 2019). All this goes on to create a hugely interdependent media ecosystem.

To conclude, one of the biggest takeaways from online movements reflects on the changing nature of activism today. No longer can a person expect to gain online traction by giving a long speech on a serious issue at a University campus or by staging a demonstration on the streets. To gain online momentum, activists need to engage with people from varied backgrounds in creative ways. Depending on the nature of the issue, they need to draw upon humor, satire, compelling narratives, powerful visuals, catchy hashtags, etc., to grab the attention of people in online forums. They also need to garner support by persuading them about the authenticity and urgency of their cause. Only then will they be able to build massive online support which will spill over to streets in the form of protests and marches that will move policy makers to take notice as ignoring such mass momentum may lead to grave consequences.

References

About. (2011). *The Occupy Solidarity Network, Inc.* Retrieved from http://occupywallst.org/about/

Allana, A. (2017). WhatsApp, crowds and power in India. *The New York Times.* Retrieved from https://www.nytimes.com/2017/06/21/opinion/whatsapp-crowds-and-power-in-india.html

Banerji, A. (2018, July 12). India scraps tax on sanitary pads in boost for girls' education. *Reuters.com.* Retrieved from https://www.reuters.com/article/india-women-sanitation/india-scraps-tax-on-sanitary-pads-in-boost-for-girls-education-idUSL8N1UG4HN

Beeston, L. (2011, October 11). The Ballerina and the Bull: Adbusters' Micah White on 'The Last Great Social Movement.' *The Link.* Retrieved fromhttps://thelinknewspaper.ca/article/the-ballerina-and-the-bull

Berrett, D. (2011, October 16). Intellectual roots of wall st. protest lie in academe. *The Chronicle of Higher Education.* Retrieved fromhttps://www.chronicle.com/article/Intellectual-Roots-of-Wall/129428

Bhattacharya, S., & Dasgupta, S. (2018). #MeToo Impact on corporate India: Women executives more confident but cautious. *The Economic Times.* Retrieved from https://economictimes.indiatimes.com/news/company/corporate-trends/metoo-impact-on-corporate-india-women-executives-more-confident-but-cautious/articleshow/66189938.cms?from=mdr

Bhushan, R. (2018). #MeToo impact: Companies tightening policy to make workplaces safer. *The Economic Times.* Retrieved from https://economictimes.indiatimes.com/news/company/corporate-trends/metoo-impact-companies-tightening-policy-to-make-workplaces-safer/articleshow/66142063.cms?from=mdr

Borissova, B. (2019, December 10). *How TikTok is becoming our go-to app for political activism.* Retrieved from https://screenshot-magazine.com/politics/tiktok-political activism-gen-z/

Carr, D. (2012, March 25). Hashtag activism, and its limits. *The New York Times.* Retrieved from https://www.nytimes.com/2012/03/26/business/media/hashtag-activism-and-its-limits.html

Chandrashekhar, A. (2019, April 17). TikTok no longer available on Google and Apple stores. *The Economic Times.* Retrieved from https://economictimes.indiatimes.com/tech/software/google-blocks-chinese-app-tiktok-in-india-after-court-order/articleshow/68916458.cms

Christensen, H. S. (2011). Political activities on the Internet: Slacktivism or political participation by other means? *First Monday, 16*. Retrieved from https://firstmo nday.org/ojs/index.php/fm/article/download/3336/2767

Couts, A. (2015). *The new era of hashtag activism*. Retrieved from https://kernelm ag.dailydot.com/issuesections/features-issuesections/11390/hashtag-activism -real/

Dasgupta, R. K. (2014). Parties, advocacy and activism: Interrogating community and class in digital queer India. In C. Pullen (Ed.), *Queer Youth and Media Cultures*. London: Palgrave Macmillan.

Day, E. (2015, July 19). #BlackLivesMatter: The birth of a new civil rights movement. *The Guardian*. Retrieved form https://www.theguardian.com/world /2015/jul/19/blacklivesmatter-birth-civil-rights-movement

Dey, A. (2020). Sites of exception: Gender violence, digital activism, and Nirbhaya's zone of anomie in India. *Violence against Women, 26*(11), 1423–1444. doi: 10.1177/1077801219862633

Diwanji, S. (2019, September 23). Number of Indian and English language internet users in India 2011–2021. *Statista.com*. Retrieved from https://www.statista .com/statistics/718420/internet-user-base-by-language-india/

Fadnis, D. (2017) Feminist activists protest tax on sanitary pads: attempts to normalize conversations about menstruation in India using hashtag activism. *Feminist Media Studies, 17*(6), 1111–1114. doi: 10.1080/14680777.2017.1380430

Fuentes, M. A. (n.d.) Digital activism. *Encyclopaedia Britannica*. Retrieved fromh ttps://www.britannica.com/topic/digital-activism

Gil, P. (2020). What is a meme? *Lifewire.com*. Retrieved from https://www.lifewire .com/what-is-a-meme-2483702

Hashmi, S. (2020, March 21). *50+ WhatsApp facts and stats that you must know in 2020*. Retrieved from https://www.connectivasystems.com/whatsapp-facts-s tats-2020/

Ice bucket challenge: What are the lessons for marketers? (2014, August 27). *The Guardian*. Retrieved from https://www.theguardian.com/media-network/media -network-blog/2014/aug/27/ice-bucket-challenge-lessons-marketing.

Jain, J. (2020). India and its #MeToo Movement in 2020: Where are we now? *Feminism II*. Retrieved from https://feminisminindia.com/2020/02/03/india-metoo-movement-2020/

Kajol shares a meme about Coronavirus safety and it has a hilarious DDLJ twist! (2020, March 13). *The Times of India*, Retrieved from https://timesofindia.indi atimes.com/entertainment/hindi/bollywood/news/kajol-shares-a-meme-about -coronavirus-safety-and-it-has-a-hilarious-ddlj-twist/articleshow/74605741.cms

Kar, S. (2020, January 30). Rise of the meme economy in India. *Economic Times*. Retrieved from https://tech.economictimes.indiatimes.com/news/internet/rise-of -the-meme-economy-in-india/73741398

Kaun, A., & Uldam, J. (2018). Digital activism: After the hype. *New Media & Society, 20*(6), 2099–2106.

Khomami, N. (2017). #MeToo: How a hashtag became a rallying cry against sexual harassment. *The Guardian*. Retrieved from https://www.theguardian.com/world /2017/oct/20/women-worldwide-use-hashtag-metoo-against-sexual-harassment

Kuo, L. (2019, November 27). TikTok 'makeup tutorial' goes viral with call to action on China's treatment of Uighurs. *The Guardian*. Retrieved from https://www.theguardian.com/technology/2019/nov/27/tiktok-makeup-tutorial-conceals-call-to-action-on-chinas-treatment-of-uighurs

Losh, E. (2014). Hashtag feminism and Twitter activism in India. *Social Epistemology Review and Reply Collective*, *3*(3), 11–22. http://wp.me/p1Bfg0-1Kx11

Mina, A. X. (2019). *Memes to movements: How the world's most viral media is changing social protest and power*. Boston, MA: Beason Press.

Mishra, S. (2019). "Tweet first, work on the story later:" Role of social media in Indian journalism. In S. Rao (Ed.), *Indian journalism in a new era: Changes, challenges, and perspectives* (pp. 140–157). New Delhi: Oxford University Press.

National Institute of Neurological Disorders and Stroke. Amyotrophic lateral sclerosis (ALS) fact sheet. (n.d.). Retrieved from https://www.ninds.nih.gov/

Neyazi, T. (2019). Internet vernacularization, mobilization and journalism. In S. Rao (Ed.), *Indian journalism in a new era: Changes, challenges, and perspectives* (pp. 95–114). New Delhi: Oxford University Press.

Ohlheiser, A. (2017, October 19). The woman behind 'Me Too' knew the power of the phrase when she created it — 10 years ago. *The Washington Post*. Retrieved from https://www.washingtonpost.com/news/the-intersect/wp/2017/10/19/the-woman-behind-me-too-knew-the-power-of-the-phrase-when-she-created-it-10-years-ago/

Parsheera, S. (2019). India's on a digital sprint that is leaving millions behind. *BBC.com*. Retrieved from https://www.bbc.com/news/world-asia-india-49085846

Price, H. (2019, November 6). TikTok activism: "We're changing the world in 15 seconds." BBC.com. Retrieved from bbc.co.uk/bbcthree/article/fa349327-bdee-489b-ae44-da4f808d82b8

Sengupta, T. (2020, March 24). PM Modi's innovative banner reminds people to stay home, wins praise on Twitter. *Hindustan Times*. Retrieved from https://www.hindustantimes.com/it-s-viral/pm-modi-announces-lockdown-shares-innovative-banner-to-remind-people-to-stay-home/story-sWNYGeLAgE1q3d9kOk5ZYM.html

Suciu, P. (2019). Is posting on social media a valid form of activism? *Forbes.com* Retrieved from https://www.forbes.com/sites/petersuciu/2019/11/01/is-posting-on-social-media-a-valid-form-of-activisim/#23567d0021cc

Sivakumar, B. (2017, January 23). Jallikattu: Tamil Nadu assembly passes bill to amend PCA Act. *The Times of India*. Retrieved from http://timesofindia.indiatimes.com/articleshow/56738068.cms?utm_source=contentofinterest&utm_medium=text&utm_campaign=cppst

Thakur, A. K. (2019). New media and the dalit counter-public sphere. *Television & New Media*, *21*(4), 360–375. doi: 10.1177/1527476419872133

The best memes and GIFs Indians are sharing to cope with the spread of coronavirus. Trends Desk (2020, March 5). *The Indian Express*. Retrieved from https://indianexpress.com/article/trending/trending-in-india/coronavirus-india-memes-and-gifs-6300404/

Udupa, S., Venkataraman, S., & Khan, A. (2020). "Millennial India": Global digital politics in context. *Television & New Media, 21*(4), 343–359.

Varadhan, S., & Kalra, A. (2019, April 3). Madras High Court asks government to ban "inappropriate" video app TikTok. *Reuters.com*. Retrieved from https://in .reuters.com/article/tiktok-india-court/indian-state-court-asks-government-to-ba n-inappropriate-video-app-tiktok-idINKCN1RF2C2

Weinstein, A. (2011). "We are the 99 percent" creators revealed. Retrieved from https://www.motherjones.com/politics/2011/10/we-are-the-99-percent-creators/

Wines, M. (2009, March 11). A dirty pun tweaks China's online censors. *The New York Times*. Retrieved from https://archive.nytimes.com/www.nytimes.com/2 009/03/12/world/asia/12beast.html

6   "Digital Detox"

Resisting the lure of the digital

What is the last thing we do before going to bed? We check our phones. Some of us even ensure our phones are kept within reach so we can stretch our hands in the middle of the night and scroll for messages. Then again, we check our phones first thing in the morning even before our eyes are fully open.

Overuse of smartphones is a highly relatable issue as most of us struggle to find experiences outside the digital realm. We strive to maintain some sort of work–life balance even as we receive and respond to work emails and WhatsApp messages from our bosses and colleagues at all hours of the day.

It is not all about work though. There are jokes, memes, and forwards of mundane things throughout the day and we respond to each one of them with appropriate emojis and comments. In fact, many of us would assume that we are unloved and forgotten by our friends if we did not receive these forwards.

We seem to enjoy interacting with the world through our digital devices until it becomes a pain in the neck, literally. So many of us have developed spondylitis and eyesight issues as we spend most of our waking moments staring at multiple screens. Our digital devices also keep us away from the people we live with.

The COVID-19 pandemic has increased our screen time exponentially. With social distancing norms in place, many are working out, cooking, and even meditating in front of a screen. Participating in dozens of video calls is leaving us exhausted and overwhelmed. The new situation has prompted many articles on ways to reduce screen time and combat "Zoom fatigue" (Fosslien & Duffy, 2020). Overall, the "new normal" imposed by the pandemic has added momentum to the digital detox movement.

What is digital detox?

The phrase "digital detox" was included in the Oxford dictionary in 2013 and refers to "a period of time during which a person refrains from using electronic devices such as smartphones or computers, regarded as an opportunity to reduce stress or focus on social interaction in the physical world."

One just needs to type the phrase "digital detox" on an online search engine to recognize the abundance of resources on this concept. Experts suggest focusing on the essentials of life, not glamourizing busy-ness, not checking our cell phones ever so often, and undertaking digital technology fasts to detox ourselves (Davis, 2018).

To reduce the use of digital devices during the pandemic, some suggest that we distinguish helpful screen time from harmful ones and opt for voice calls instead of video calls to reduce technology-related anxiety and stress (Holland, 2020).

Reading literature on how to do a digital detox feels very much like reading a manual on any form of drug addiction. For instance, one such how-to-detox article suggests finding a "detox buddy" with whom we can discuss our detox journey, support one another, and make progress, one device at a time (Wells, 2016).

Drawing upon analysis of digital detox–promoting texts including self-help literature, memoirs, and corporate websites, researchers at the University of Oslo, Norway, identified three dominant themes: descriptions about losing a sense of time and place and damaging one's physical and mental health (Syvertsen & Enli, 2020). Many consider time spent on social media as "wasted time" and view digital devices as a drain on our "real-life" relationships. Almost all of us have experienced instances where we click on a link because we want to take a short break from work but end up clicking on a series of subsequent links.

Digital detox texts often offer practical tips such as replacing our mobile phones with an old-fashioned alarm clock and demarcating screen-free times and zones. They also offer more philosophical advice such as living in the present moment, enjoying a walk or a sunset and getting to know oneself. To tackle physical and mental ailments arising out of excessive use of digital media, digital detox enthusiasts recommend we eat, sleep, exercise, and nurture our "authentic" selves (Syvertsen & Enli, 2020).

Searching for authenticity, focus, and meaning

Contemporary society displays a yearning for an "authentic life" (Syvertsen & Enli, 2020). Authenticity, in this case, is often defined as life that is not tied to social media platforms, apps, and digital devices. The assumption is that social media and digital devices render our lives superficial and do not let us connect with people in person.

Sherry Turkle, a professor at the Massachusetts Institute of Technology, in her books *Alone Together* (2011) and *Reclaiming Conversation* (2015) takes a similar stand and highlights the adverse impacts of digital technology on our lives and relationships. In the latter book, Turkle asks readers to "put technology in its place and reclaim conversation" (p. 25). She also offers examples of how technology often gets in the way of conversation.

Turkle makes a compelling argument about people being "partially present" when interacting with others because they are always multitasking with digital devices. While this may be true, the binary Turkle presents between technology usage and having a good conversation may not apply to everyone. Technology can both facilitate and interrupt conversation. It depends on how we use it and when.

Moreover, one cannot assume that all face-to-face conversations are authentic in nature. Erving Goffman in his 1956 book *The Presentation of Self in Everyday Life* used the imagery of a theatre to describe our everyday social interactions. He wrote about the various roles we perform by managing impressions in the front stage of our lives while being our relaxed selves backstage. We behave differently in front of an audience than how we do alone.

Whether we believe we are more authentic online or offline, the need for digital detox in most people does not emanate from a search for authenticity alone. It also emerges from a practical need to do focused work without distractions.

In his book *Deep Work*, computer scientist Cal Newport (2016) argues that modern knowledge workers are losing their ability to do focused work over long periods of time as they are continually distracted by their digital devices. After establishing the value of focused work, Newport asks us to quit social media, embrace boredom, and reduce the amount of shallow work we do so we can focus on what is really important. He defines shallow work as "noncognitively demanding, logistical-style tasks, often performed while distracted" (p. 228).

In many of us, the need for digital detox emerges from a feeling of anxiety about losing control over our own attention. It has led to the emergence of podcasts, shows, and workshops on digital decluttering that manage to get a lot of traction. For instance, former BBC reporter Manoush Zomorodi's podcasts on preserving humanity in the digital age called "Note to Self" on New York Public Radio managed to get a lot of attention from listeners.

The podcasts covered highly relatable topics such as creative burnout, information overload, and digital privacy, amongst others. They guided listeners on ways to decrease their dependency on digital devices, platforms, and apps. Zomorodi's 2015 book *Bored and Brilliant: How Spacing Out Can Unlock Your Most Productive and Creative Self* is based on an experiment she conducted with her podcast listeners.

Inside a digital detox retreat

Media reports highlight a growing interest in "digital-free tourism" which involves holidays in places where Wi-Fi signals are absent or controlled (Li et al., 2018). Such environments may include natural, remote areas, specific resorts, and restaurants that do not offer Wi-Fi access, amongst others.

Not everyone believes that taking a short break from digital devices in a remote location will help. Miriam Rasch (2017), a researcher at the Institute of Network Cultures in Amsterdam, describes digital detox as "the carrot in front of the donkey's nose." She argues that taking a short break from our digital devices only helps ensure that we remain tied to them in the long run. According to her, digital detox exercises merely fight the symptoms, not the cause. Because after spending time in the woods at a retreat, we have to get back to our routines – and our devices.

Theodora Sutton, a digital anthropologist at the Oxford Internet Institute, conducted fieldwork at a digital detox retreat in California and found that most of the attendees belonged to socioeconomically privileged sections of society who could afford to take leave from work and attend the retreat. They had strong views on the right usage of digital technology that echoed "Californian countercultural sentiments." After attending the retreat, they resolved to use their digital devices purposefully rather than engage in unnecessary browsing.

The attendees also idealized face-to-face communication over online socializing. Such a romantic notion of offline interactions may lead us to idealize "family time" while ignoring ground realities (Sutton, 2020).

Lockdowns introduced during the COVID-19 pandemic have shown that not everyone has an enjoyable time when they are locked at home with their families over a long period of time. Many sought comfort and solace in online connections. Moreover, social media platforms are often used to keep in touch with people who are already a part of our offline lives.

Instead of blindly blaming digital technology, Sutton recommends we focus less on technology and the concept of "addiction" and more on "how our cultural values and beliefs interweave and collide with everyday digital use" (Sutton, 2020, p. 22). Basically, we need to question why and how our values make us perceive a certain usage of digital technology as harmful and for whom.

While previous research indicated that social media activity is often perceived as performative in nature, more recent literature suggests that the blurring of boundaries between our offline and online lives has led to many people viewing both as authentic and meaningful (Syvertsen & Enli, 2020). For instance, Chapter 1 of this book highlighted how some people presented what they believed was their authentic self in the form of alternative selfies such as illness selfie, domestic violence selfie, nude selfie, etc.

Individual efforts at digital detox

People have found innovative ways to reduce screen time. For instance, a senior academic at a well-known school of management in western India does not open WhatsApp forwards unless it is accompanied by a memo explaining why that particular video or image is being sent to him. His technique has worked so far as few send him videos and images anymore.

Interestingly, many today rely on apps to beat digital distractions. Based on a study with young adults, Desirée Schmuck, a Munich-based media researcher, found that usage of digital detox apps can reduce compulsive smartphone usage. These digital detox apps monitor users' smartphone usage and nudge them to disconnect from their digital devices for specific durations (Schmuck, 2020).

Some people also express their resistance against excessive use of ICTs by creating images to highlight their cause and posting them online (Gomez et al., 2015). A study that examined images of resistance to ICTs revealed that while some images were subtle, others presented their message in a dramatic way. For instance, images that highlighted addiction to technology showed a woman snorting cocaine arranged to spell out "Facebook," syringes to be injected with logos of different social media on them, cigarettes to be smoked, etc.

Some images used humor to communicate their message and make an impact. While most of the images focused on negative consequences of technology use such as addition, physical and mental health issues, loss of relationships, etc., a few focused on the positive things that could be gained by resisting digital technology such as peace of mind and a deeper connect with nature (Gomez et al., 2015).

Laura Portwood-Stacer, a researcher at New York University, interviewed people who opted out of Facebook and examined the ways in which they presented their decisions, tastes, and preferences as distinct from mainstream discourses on social media activity. For instance, many said they did not want to waste their time on Facebook, especially when they had fulfilling "real" lives. They positioned themselves as making more "authentic" choices as they would rather read a book, enjoy a glass of wine or meet with people rather than spend time on Facebook. They also highlighted how their productivity had increased after opting out of Facebook.

However, they also claimed that their choices were not viewed favourably by many of their friends, who considered it a ploy to get more attention or a display of self-righteousness and elitism. Those who claimed to opt out of Facebook for political or ideological reasons rarely managed to get support of their friends. Meanwhile, those who claimed to leave Facebook for personal reasons such as avoiding an ex after a breakup received sympathy and understanding.

The study also revealed that those who are interested in building collective resistance against social media culture need to ensure that their decisions are perceived as relatable. Without making such an effort, individual refusal alone may not serve as an effective strategy of political engagement in the case of social media (Portwood-Stacer, 2012).

Legislation on the right to disconnect

It is paradoxical that we have to make a personal and individual attempt to "detox" while governments and corporations are moving most things online through various digitization projects. While the digital detox movement targets individual lifestyle changes, it does not give adequate importance to structural and systemic changes such as a change in the workplace email policies or curb employee exploitation through expectations of constant connectivity.

France set a new trend when it enforced the "El Khomri Law" or the right to disconnect from work calls and emails in off-duty hours in the year 2017. The law is named after the country's then Labor Minister, Myriam El Khomri. In July 2018, in what is considered its first public enforcement, the French Supreme Court ordered a British pest control company to pay 60,000 Euros to its former France-based employee as he had been required to constantly be on call (Ornstein & Glassberg, 2019).

After France, several countries have either enacted or considered introducing similar laws (Ornstein & Glassberg, 2019). In the Indian context, Surpiya Sule, a member of Parliament, introduced a similar Right to Disconnect Bill in the Lok Sabha in 2019. However, the chances of the bill being discussed in the Lok Sabha and becoming an Act are remote since it is a private member's bill (TNN, 2019).

Tellingly, the French law gave employees the right to disconnect but did not explicitly define it. Instead it obligated employers to delineate the specifics in consultation with employees. As countries consider such legislation, they will need to determine how to implement the law across various sectors which have varying requirements from employees. They also need to ensure that employees do not end up spending longer hours at work just to exercise their right to disconnect during off-duty hours (Ornstein & Glassberg, 2019).

While legislation can address work-related digital communication overload, reducing personal engagement with digital devices will require individual effort. Thus, we need a combination of state, organizational, and individual effort if we want to reduce the overwhelming presence of digital devices in our lives.

The way forward

In times to come, it is important that we locate resistance to digital technologies within the history of human resistance to new technologies and inventions including telephones, television, cinema, etc. (Syvertsen & Enli, 2020).

We also need to acknowledge the diversity of experiences people have with digital media. Not everyone views digital media as a toxic thing. While some may find their offline interactions as more authentic than their online ones, others may have a completely different perspective. The fact is what comprises an authentic human life is a highly debatable topic. It is difficult for anyone to cast a judgment or define its boundaries.

We must also exercise caution while reading sensational media reports about the impacts of digital media on mental health. Although such reports highlight the dangers of digital technology, we should remember that the Diagnostic and Statistical Manual of Mental Disorders does not recognize the term "Internet addiction" (Sutton, 2020). Hence, we need to exercise care when we borrow terms from the mental health sciences to describe everyday behaviors we observe amongst people.

Finally, we need to recognize that not every person has the social capital and economic privilege to unplug their lives. Many are not ready to bear the economic, social, personal, and psychological costs of opting out of digital platforms and devices. In such a context, the way forward may just lie in being selective about what gets our attention. Moderating our digital pursuits may be the answer we are looking for.

References

Davis, T. (2018). 5 ways to do a digital detox. *Psychology Today*. Retrieved from https://www.psychologytoday.com/us/blog/click-here-happiness/201801/5-ways-do-digital-detox

Fosslien, L., & Duffy, M. W. (2020). How to combat Zoom fatigue. *Harvard Business Review*. Retrieved from https://hbr.org/2020/04/how-to-combat-zoom-fatigue

Gomez, R., Foot, K., Young, M., Paquet-Kinsley, R., & Morrison, S. (2015). Pulling the plug visually: Images of resistance to ICTs and connectivity. *First Monday*, *20*(11), doi: 10.5210/fm.v20i11.6286

Holland, M. (2020). How to take a digital detox during the Covid-19 pandemic. *BBC.com*. Retrieved from https://www.bbc.com/worklife/article/20200513-how-to-take-a-digital-detox-during-the-covid-19-pandemic

Li, J., Pearce, P. L., & Low, D. (2018). Media representations of digital-free tourism: A critical discourse analysis. *Tourism Management, 69*, 317–329.

Newport, C. (2016). *Deep work*. London: Piatkus.

Ornstein, D., & Glassberg, J. B. (2019). More countries consider implementing a "Right to Disconnect." *The National Law Review*. Retrieved from https://www.natlawreview.com/article/more-countries-consider-implementing-right-to-disconnect

Portwood-Stacer, L. (2012). Media refusal as conspicuous non-consumption: The performative and political dimensions of Facebook abstention. *New Media & Society, 15*(7), 1041–1057.

Rasch, M. D. (2017). *Notes on digital detox*. Institute of Network Cultures. Retrieved from networkcultures.org/blog/2017/11/21/notes-on-digital-detox/

Schmuck, D. (2020). Does digital detox work? Exploring the role of digital detox applications for problematic smartphone use and well-being of young adults using multigroup analysis. *Cyberpsychology, Behavior, and Social Networking, 23*(8), 526–532. doi: 10.1089/cyber.2019.0578

Sutton, T. (2020). Digital harm and addiction: An anthropological view. *Anthropology Today, 36*(1), 17–22.

Syvertsen, T., & Enli, G. (2019). Digital detox: Media resistance and the promise of authenticity. *Convergence: The International Journal of Research into New Media Technologies, 26*(5–6), 1269–1283. doi: 10.1177/1354856519847325

Times News Network. (2019). The bill will give you the right to ignore your boss (after work!). *The Times of India*. Retrieved from https://timesofindia.indiatimes.com/home/sunday-times/this-bill-will-give-you-the-right-to-ignore-your-boss-after-work/articleshow/67509210.cms

Turkle, S. (2015). *Reclaiming conversation*. New York: Penguin.

Wells, J. (2016). 9 ways to start (and stick to) a digital detox. *The Telegraph*. Retrieved from https://www.telegraph.co.uk/better/technology/9-ways-to-start-and-stick-to-a-digital-detox/

Zomorodi, M. (n.d.). *Note to self*. WNYC Studios. Retrieved from https://www.wnycstudios.org/podcasts/notetoself

Conclusion

The COVID-19 pandemic has introduced massive changes in digital cultures across the globe. With draconian restrictions and multiple lockdowns in many countries, much of the world seems to have moved online. We work online. We study online. We order food online. We find partners online. We entertain ourselves online.

But it is not just the way we live that has suddenly changed. The COVID-19 pandemic has also changed the way we die. The virus no longer lets people die surrounded by their family and friends. Instead, it forces people to die alone – surrounded by strangers, if at all – and often attached to a ventilator for respiratory support.

Consequently, digital cultures surrounding death and dying are also changing. In such dire times, more people are attending virtual "death cafes" where they can discuss their fears about death during the pandemic and plan their final hours. They get a chance to express their anxieties and take critical decisions about possible hospitalization, ventilator support, and even their funerals (Brooks, 2020).

Taking such steps probably gives participants a sense of control over things that they have absolutely no control over. According to death and grieving researcher David Kessler, death cafes give people a forum to share their deepest fears (WLNS, 2020).

It would be wrong to assume that any discussion about death is necessarily morbid. In fact, the death café Facebook Page strives to keep an upbeat mood about the inevitable end of our lives. For instance, a meme with skeletons dancing in the graveyard carried the following text: "When the 'g' falls off the graveyard sign." Another post declared, "Just as talking about sex won't make you pregnant, talking about death won't make you dead – Jon Underwood."

In fact, humor plays a big role in digital cultures. Memes, hashtags, and short video clips often aim for the funny bone of users. However, one should not assume that they are superficial in nature. Some deliver profound messages garbed in humor and sarcasm. Engaging creatively and consistently with users requires a good understanding of what they perceive as authentic, credible, and funny – an issue discussed elaborately in several chapters.

This book has focused on people's interactions with digital technology in various aspects of their lives. It has explored multiple digital practices including methods of self-presentation on social media platforms; intimacy and infidelity in digital spaces; digital healthcare and the self-tracking movement; techniques adopted by Internet celebrities and the nature of Internet fame; digital activism; and digital detox. My sincere hope is that the reader will use the insights on digital cultures presented in this book as a user or creator of a digital service or product.

Overall, the chapters in this book make three main arguments: Rather than drawing generic conclusions, it is important to explore specific contexts of users, their nuanced goals, and alternative interpretations of standard practices to get an in-depth understanding of digital cultures. It may be erroneous to hold extreme views and assume either highly utopian or dystopian consequences of digital technology usage. The way people use technology will always be dynamic and contextual. This is the reason, as argued in Chapter 1, it is important to go beyond mainstream online identities such as those on Facebook and Instagram and explore pseudonymous and anonymous online environments where the pressure to perform and conform would be less.

Secondly, instead of attributing sole causality to digital technology, it is imperative to understand the dynamic and complex ways in which people interact with digital devices, tools, and apps, and recognize the ways in which they mutually influence one another. For instance, we cannot hold digital technology responsible for Indian matrimonial sites including caste and sub-caste categories for people looking for spouses.

Similarly, we cannot simply blame dating apps for extra-marital affairs: It is the app users who decided to seek romance and intimacy outside their primary relationship. Digital technology may have facilitated infidelity, on the one hand, and partner surveillance, on the other, but it is not solely responsible for these changes. Thus, we must focus on the existing and emerging needs, wants, and desires of people. Awareness of people's emotions, attitudes, and contexts is critical.

Thirdly, the chapters in this book emphasize that the way in which we balance our quest for convenience with our need for privacy will deeply influence the nature of usage of digital technology in the future. Businesses will strive to offer more personalized experiences to users as they will have more information on every aspect of their lives. Those companies who can get users to trust them so that they willingly share their private information will emerge winners in this race (Marr, 2019).

The experience will be unique for each one of us as privacy means different things to different people. While some of us are more willing to share our personal information for the sake of convenience, others are cautious about third-party data sharing and increased surveillance by governments and corporations alike.

With the establishment of European Union's General Data Protection Regulation and global pressure on technology companies to ensure privacy of users, digital privacy is likely to become a key brand differentiator (Newman, 2020). Will tech giants become more transparent and allow users to opt out of data collection schemes or will they find new ways to hide their data gathering methods? The answer to that question will determine the future of our digital privacy.

But whatever a company's stand on digital privacy, they will need to improve data security as breaches continue to compromise user safety. In July 2020, for instance, Twitter accounts of several public figures including Barack Obama, Joe Biden, Kanye West, Elon Musk, Jeff Bezos, and Bill Gates were hacked as part of a Bitcoin scam (BBC, 2020). All tech firms and social media companies must prioritize cybersecurity as such incidents can cause substantial damage. With content on social media platforms influencing electoral outcomes, the impact of a breach may not be just financial in nature. It could be political, social, and deeply personal as well.

However, it's not just the responsibility of organizations to ensure cybersecurity by protecting against botnet attacks, ransomware, phishing attacks, trojan, data breaches, etc. (Mathur, 2020). Data protection must be ensured at the individual level as well. Downloading malicious apps, using faulty Internet connections, not protecting our personal information including passwords, location data, private photos and login credentials adequately will only lead to more identity thefts and digital fraud.

Digital privacy scholars point out that while many of us express concern about our privacy online, our actions do not match the statements we make as only few amongst us take security measures on their digital devices (Bongiovanni et al., 2020). Dubbed the "privacy paradox," this phenomenon presents a major obstacle for ensuring digital privacy at the individual level.

Safeguarding our personal information will become even more important as we move into an era of AI companionship. More importantly, as we become more comfortable communicating and confiding with our robots and digital assistants, will we be less open and trusting of other humans (Christakis, 2019)? AI experts believe things could go either way. Robots could help humans relate better or jeopardize human relations.

While we still cannot predict the details, we do know that AI will impact our experiences of love, friendship, cooperation, kindness, generosity, etc., in complex ways. For instance, since digital devices and robots will be programmed to tell us what we want to hear, one wonders if it will reduce our capacity to tolerate life's disappointments (Christakis, 2019). Experts recommend that we exercise great caution while introducing AI in our lives. Organizations need to consider their impact not just on individuals but on society and humanity at large.

Finally, even as we make rapid advancements in the digital world, we need to remember that sudden digital transitions often reinforce digital divides. For instance, Indian news media reported incidents of students committing suicide as they did not own smartphones and computers and could not attend online classes during the COVID-19 pandemic (Babu, 2020; Times News Network, 2020).

To prevent such grave casualties, we need to develop a more inclusive approach toward digital transformation. Mere advancements in digital technology will not improve most people's lives. The future lies in the hope that digital technology will leave no one behind.

References

Babu, R. (2020, June 2). Kerala girl allegedly kills self for missing online classes, Rahul Gandhi offers help. *Hindustan Times*. Retrieved from https://www.hindustantimes.com/india-news/kerala-girl-allegedly-commits-suicide-for-missing-online-classes-mp-rahul-gandhi-offers-help/story-RbYEOiznZWZPfvELnEkGwI.html

Bongiovanni, I., Renaud, K., & Alesia, N. (2020). The privacy paradox: We claim we care about our data, so why don't our actions match? *The Conversation*. Retrieved from https://theconversation.com/the-privacy-paradox-we-claim-we-care-about-our-data-so-why-dont-our-actions-match-143354

British Broadcasting Corporation. (2020, July 16). Major US Twitter accounts hacked in Bitcoin scam. *BBC.com*. Retrieved from https://www.bbc.com/news/technology-53425822

Brooks, L. (2020, April 13). Death cafes report surge of interest since Covid-19 outbreak. *Guardian.com*. Retrieved from https://www.theguardian.com/society/2020/apr/13/death-cafes-see-surge-of-interest-in-online-events

Christakis, N. A. (2019). How AI will rewire us. *Atlantic.com*. Retrieved from https://www.theatlantic.com/magazine/archive/2019/04/robots-human-relationships/583204/

Marr, B. (2019). The 5 biggest future technology trends: Accenture reveals their vision of post-digital. *Forbes.com*. Retrieved from https://www.forbes.com/sites/bernardmarr/2019/03/07/the-5-biggest-future-technology-trends-accenture-reveals-their-vision-of-post-digital/#14374a67131d

Mathur, N. (2020). NortonLifeLockon changing threat landscape, protecting data, top cyber threats, and more. *Mashable.com*. Retrieved from https://in.mashable.com/tech/16218/nortonlifelock-on-changing-threat-landscape-protecting-data-top-cyber-threats-and-more

Newman, D. (2020). Top 10 digital transformation trends for 2020. *Forbes.com*. Retrieved from https://www.forbes.com/sites/danielnewman/2019/07/14/top -10-digital-transformation-trends-for-2020/#12a200e076be

Times News Network. (2020, June 20). West Bengal: Unable to attend online classes, Howrah girl kills self. *The Times of India*. Retrieved from https://timesof india.indiatimes.com/city/kolkata/unable-to-attend-online-classes-girl-kills-self/ articleshowprint/76473056.cms

WLNS. (2020, July 31). Growing trend of death cafes. Retrieved from https://www .wlns.com/news/growing-trend-of-death-cafes/?fbclid=IwAR2gEDw2eCezv9S lTP6_9-zBZEi6p9lbf3_FxuZZPrt1ydFf-NHorMqnBVc

Index

For Product Safety Concerns and Information please contact our EU
representative GPSR@taylorandfrancis.com
Taylor & Francis Verlag GmbH, Kaufingerstraße 24, 80331 München, Germany